DeVǫTiǫNS FǫR PEǫPLE WHǫ LǫVE KiDS

20 Team-Builders for Children's Ministry

by Gordon and Becki West

Group
Loveland, Colorado

Devotions for People Who Love Kids:
20 Team-Builders for Children's Ministry

Credits

Editor: Michele B. Buckingham
Book Acquisitions Editor: Lori Haynes Niles
Chief Creative Officer: Joani Schultz
Copy Editor: Bob Kretschman
Art Director: Kari K. Monson
Designer: Eris Klein
Cover Art Director: Jeff A. Storm
Cover Designer: Becky Hawley
Cover Photographer: Craig DeMartino
Computer Graphic Artist: Joyce Douglas
Illustrators: Kathy Benson, Tony Caldwell, and Eris Klein
Production Manager: Peggy Naylor

Library of Congress Cataloging-in-Publication Data
West, Gordon, 1959-
    Devotions for people who love kids : 20 team-builders for children's ministry / by Gordon and Becki West.
    p.   cm.
    Includes index.
    ISBN 0-7644-2115-8 (alk. paper)
    1. Church work with children–Prayer-books and devotions–English.
I. West, Becki, 1955- . II. Title.
BV639.C4W47   1999
242' .89–dc21   98-53165
                                                  CIP

10 9 8 7 6 5 4 3 2 1   08 07 06 05 04 03 02 01 00 99
Printed in the United States of America.

contents

INTRODUCTION

"Thank you for encouraging me and helping me remember why I first started teaching kids," the note read. "I was ready to quit, but today's workshop touched my heart. Now I know I can keep going—for the kids and for God."

That message is typical of many that we receive from volunteer children's workers after leading teacher-training workshops in churches throughout the country. People constantly tell us that they were on the verge of giving up, but when their hearts were encouraged, they knew they should—and could—keep going.

It's not that we do anything so special in our training sessions. It's just that we try to remember one thing that many churches seem to forget: People in children's ministry need to hear that they're doing well, that they're appreciated, and that what they're doing is important. They may know these things in their hearts. But like all of us, they want—they *need*—to hear that someone else knows it, too!

Use the devotional ideas in the following pages as you prepare for teacher planning meetings or special events designed to encourage or motivate your children's staff. As a special feature, each devotional includes "Words to Encourage People Who Love Kids"—a specific message intended to touch the hearts of your volunteers. You will repeat these encouraging words several times in each session as you lead, inspire, and challenge your teachers both from your heart and from the Word of God.

In addition to twenty complete devotionals that are appropriate for many different purposes and occasions, we have included a section with another twenty-one "bonus ideas" for challenging and affirming your children's team. Don't be afraid to dream! Maybe an idea in this book will serve as a springboard for an even better idea of your own.

We've also included a section of sixteen photocopiable postcards—we call them "Love Notes"—that you can use to encourage your workers from time to time. These can serve as quick, tangible reminders of your appreciation. You'll be amazed at how your teachers will tuck these cards into their purses or display them on bulletin boards so that your words continue to affirm for weeks and months to come!

Remember: The teachers and helpers in your children's ministry are the treasures God has entrusted to your care for the work of teaching and leading children into a vital relationship with Jesus Christ. With you, these ministers have a vital role in building up the church, as Ephesians 4:11-12 tells us. Encourage them. Appreciate them. Inspire them. Love the people in your church who love kids!

1

Devotions for Ministry Leaders

♥ A Year's Worth of Encouragement

Use this devotion at a meeting of your children's ministry leaders to plan a full year's worth of creative ideas that will encourage and nurture your volunteers. Allow approximately twenty minutes.

Words to Encourage People Who Love Kids

God will use—and multiply!—everything you invest in the lives of your volunteers.

The Bible Basis

"His master replied, 'Well done, good and faithful servant! You have been faithful with a few things; I will put you in charge of many things. Come and share your master's happiness!' " (Matthew 25:23).

PREPARE FOR THIS SESSION

● Read the parable of the talents in Matthew 25:14-30. Think about the "talents" God has given you. How are you investing them?

● Watch for ways that your leaders already are encouraging others. For example, you may see a lead teacher explaining how to use the curriculum, writing a note of encouragement to a new volunteer, or stepping in to help a worker put up classroom decorations. Be ready to share several examples.

● Gift-wrap a box and its lid separately so the lid can be removed. Place enough foil-covered chocolate coins (or bright, shiny pennies) inside the box to ensure that each person in attendance will have one. (If your group is larger than twelve, prepare a box for each group of three or four people.)

● Set up your room with a chalkboard, a dry-erase

LEADER TIP:

Remember that approximate times for devotions do not include snack time. Snacks can be served after the devotion or at another appropriate point in your meeting.

board, an overhead projector, or a flip chart (plus chalk or markers) for brainstorming ideas.

● Decorate by placing a piggy bank on each table and scattering chocolate coins or pennies around each bank.

● Buy extra chocolate coins or 100 Grand candy bars to serve as your snack.

A Job Well Done

Start this session by enthusiastically sharing several examples of ways you've seen your leaders encouraging and nurturing other workers in children's ministry at your church. Tell your leaders how much you appreciate the wonderful job they do.

 Say: <u>God will use—and multiply!—everything you invest in the lives of your volunteers.</u>

A Biblical Challenge

Say: **Think about all of the volunteers that you supervise or coordinate, while I read to you a modern-day parable adapted from Matthew 25:14-30.**

Read: **Investing in volunteers is like the pastor going on a vacation who called his church leaders together and entrusted his ministry to them. To one he gave five willing volunteers, to another two volunteers, and to another one volunteer. Then he went on his vacation.**

The leader who received five volunteers immediately challenged them to grow spiritually, grouped them into ministry teams, and invested his heart and life in their well-being. Those five volunteers were so encouraged and empowered that they not only fulfilled their ministry roles, but their joy in ministry also attracted five more willing volunteers!

Similarly the leader who received two volunteers formed friendships with them and met regularly for training and planning, prayer, and study. Through their enthusiasm, he gained two more volunteers to do the work of the ministry.

But the man who received one volunteer found a hole in the ministry and stuck the volunteer in it, covering him over with tasks he was neither trained for, equipped for, nor interested in.

After a long time (especially for the guy buried in the hole!), the pastor returned and asked the church leaders what they had done with the willing volunteers that had been entrusted to them.

The leader who had been given one volunteer answered, "I was so desperate to fill the vacancy in my program that I plugged the volunteer in immediately without stopping to consider what he wanted to do or what he would be good at doing. Unfortunately, that volunteer turned out

to be pretty flaky and quit a couple of weeks later, saying he would never serve in *my* ministry again. Go figure!"

Next the two church leaders who had invested in their volunteers by loving and nurturing them told the pastor about the many blessings they had experienced because their volunteers had taken "ownership" of the ministry and had raised it to new heights through their enthusiasm and creativity.

And the pastor said, "Well done, good and faithful servants! You have been faithful with a few volunteers; you shall be put in charge of many. For everyone who invests in his volunteers will be given more, and he will have an abundance in blessed ministry."

You see, <u>God will use—and multiply!—everything you invest in the lives of your volunteers.</u>

Read: **But for the one who merely plugs holes, even those volunteers he has will quit! And he will be thrown outside into the darkness of unending hole-plugging where there will be weeping and gnashing of teeth.**

Ask:

● **Which leader do you want to be like? Why?**

● **Are the volunteers you supervise really *yours?*** (They're God's!)

● **God is the one who gives us the volunteers for our ministry. How should this knowledge affect the way we appreciate and utilize our workers?**

Twelve Months of Nurture

Say: **We want our teachers and helpers to know that they're not just plugging a hole in our ministry. By loving and working with kids, they're filling an exciting and important role. But sometimes, because they work individually in their classrooms away from the rest of the church, they may feel as if no one cares about them or even notices what they do. Let's come up with a plan to make sure our teachers and helpers know that we love them and appreciate everything they do for the children.**

Step 1—Have participants form groups of three or four with one person as the facilitator (to keep the discussion moving), one person as the recorder (to take notes), and one person as the reporter (to share ideas with the large group later). If the group has a fourth person, he or she can be the cheerleader who says, "Good idea!"

Say: **Now, in your small groups, brainstorm and think of as many creative ways as you can to show appreciation to your workers.**

Share one or more of these ideas as illustrations of what you are looking for:

● Take a flower to each teacher one Sunday;

● Write personal notes to each worker;

● Have kids write notes or draw pictures for their teachers;

● Create a "Wall of Fame" with each volunteer's photograph attached to a large construction paper star. Write one positive quality or ministry accomplishment below each picture, along with the person's name and ministry position.

Say: **Remember, in this first step, let's only share ideas. We'll evaluate them later.** Give everyone five minutes to come up with as many ideas as possible.

Step 2—Ask the facilitators to help their groups review their lists and pick the best two or three ideas. Then have the reporters share these ideas with the whole group as you record them on the board, overhead projector or flip chart.

Step 3—Say: **Now let's pick our twelve favorite ideas and make plans to implement them in the next twelve months. We'll use one idea for each month of the next year.**

Make a simple chart listing the twelve months and the encouragement idea selected for each month. Ask for a different volunteer to coordinate each project.

Say: **God will use—and multiply!—everything you invest in the lives of your volunteers.**

Good as Gold

If you have more than twelve participants, have them remain in their small groups. Otherwise, have the groups come back together at this point.

Hold up the gift-wrapped box containing the gold chocolate coins or bright pennies. Say: **Each one of you is in the business of nurturing others in the children's ministry, using your God-given gifts and talents to invest in their lives. I want you to know that I appreciate you—and so do other people. We're going to take turns now recognizing how God is working in each of your lives.**

Open the box, take out one coin or penny, and give it to one of your leaders. Tell the whole group how you have seen God working through this person to nurture other volunteers (for example, by coming in early to help a worker set up a classroom, praying with a new volunteer, or substituting in a class for a teacher who needed a break).

Say: [name], **God will use—and multiply!—everything you invest in the lives of your volunteers.**

Then pass the box to that person and say: **Now you take a turn affirming someone else.** Allow members of the group to continue to pass the box and hand out coins in this fashion until everyone has been affirmed and encouraged. (For more than twelve participants, give a box of coins to each facilitator and have them start the process within their own small groups.)

If your leaders don't know one another well enough to be able to think of specific, affirming things to say, ask them to simply hand out a coin and repeat:

"[name], **God will use—and multiply!—everything you invest in the lives of your volunteers.**"

Talking With God

Say: **Look at your coin now. Think about the investment in your volunteers it represents. As we pray silently, ask God to help you encourage and nurture your teachers and helpers.**

After several minutes, close the prayer: **Thank you, God, that you will use—and multiply!—everything we invest in the lives of _your_ volunteers. Amen.**

♥ The Harvest is Plentiful (So Why Are the Workers So Few?)

Use this devotion at a meeting of your leaders to help free them from the burden of recruiting new volunteers—and to excite them about their role in bringing in God's harvest among the children. Allow approximately twenty minutes.

Words to Encourage People Who Love Kids

*God is the Lord of the harvest. We need to ask him, and he **will** send his workers!*

The Bible Basis

"He told them, 'The harvest is plentiful, but the workers are few. Ask the Lord of the harvest, therefore, to send out workers into his harvest field' " (Luke 10:2).

PREPARE FOR THIS SESSION

● Read Luke 10:2. Think about how this verse applies to finding new volunteers for the children's ministry at your church.

● Ask one person to be a "mime" for a skit. Pick someone who you know will have fun improvising a role on the spot.

● Gather your supplies: one small paper cup or inexpensive clay pot and saucer for each participant, several packs of seeds, some small gardening shovels or spoons, and a bag of potting soil. You can also use background music such as the song "In My Garden" by Mary Rice Hopkins (from the cassette or CD *In My Garden: Sowing Seeds of Love)*.

● Print the text of 1 Thessalonians 5:24 ("The one who calls you is faithful and he will do it"), and make copies for each participant.

● Snack and decorating tips:

✱ In spring or summer, decorate your tables and meeting room with gardening supplies and tools. Arrange hand gardening tools, a few silk flowers, an assortment of seed packets—all tied up with a big raffia bow—in flower pots. Serve something "yummy" that is in season in your area (such as fresh strawberries), or toss a fruit salad and have fresh veggies and dip.

✱ In fall or winter, make a display of dried or paper leaves, and use pumpkins or squash for centerpieces. Serve harvest corn or pumpkin bread for a snack.

The Harvest in Action

Say: **I want to tell you a story about a little boy named Jerry and his special garden. You can watch this story unfold as I read.** Call the "mime" to the front to act out the part of Jerry. As you proceed through the story, pause long enough between sentences to allow "Jerry" to improvise his actions.

Read: **Jerry was ten years old when his father said he could grow his own garden. Jerry was so excited!**

First, Jerry went to the store to find just the right seeds. He picked out his favorite packets and took them home.

Then he went outside and found just the right place in the yard to dig...and dig...and dig. Soon his enthusiasm started to wane, however, as he began to get hot and tired from the hard work of preparing the soil to receive the seeds.

Still, Jerry stuck with it and planted the seeds, warm and snug, in the dirt. Again, Jerry was excited and sat back to wait for his garden to grow.

Soon Jerry saw little green things growing in his garden, but they turned out to be *weeds!* Gardening, Jerry discovered, involves lots of hard work. He pulled each of the weeds and continued to water the seeds every day.

There were disappointing days for Jerry—that first morning after planting the seeds, when he ran out to see what had sprouted and found nothing; the day he discovered the radishes had been eaten by some undetected bugs; the time the family dog decided to bury a bone under the tomatoes.

But despite all the heartache, Jerry discovered the joy of harvesting. After weeks and weeks of hard work, the little seeds finally became fully grown plants that bore fruits and vegetables. Jerry pulled a carrot from his garden and tasted it. It was much better than any carrot he had ever eaten from a store!

Jerry thanked his father for letting him grow his very own garden.

As your mime finishes and returns to the group, lead everyone in a round of applause.

Say: **The Bible talks about a harvest, too.**

Read aloud Luke 10:2. Ask:

● **How is growing a garden like working in the children's ministry?** (It's hard work; problems come along to undermine our efforts; some "seeds" sprout slowly or don't seem to make it to fruition; there are disappointments, but there is also great joy in the harvest.)

● **Is it easy or hard for you to believe that God will send out the workers into his harvest? Explain.**

● **If it's God's harvest and he is the one who sends out the workers, what is our part?** (Ask him for workers; ask people to work!)

Say: **Whether we are growing a garden or ministering to young lives, the harvest is God's responsibility. Ultimately, only he can cause the growth. Only he can deliver the crop. And only he can provide the workers!**

God is the Lord of the harvest. We need to ask him, and he _will_ send his workers!

Planting Seeds for the Harvest

Give each participant a paper cup (or clay pot and saucer). Have them spoon a little potting soil into the cup and plant a few seeds. "In My Garden" can be played as background music, if it is available.

Say: **These seeds are for you to take home. You will need to water them and take care of them, but ultimately, _God_ will make them grow. Keep your plant as a reminder that you are in ministry because God sent you into his harvest field—and he is the one who will send more workers into the harvest.**

God is the Lord of the harvest. We need to ask him, and he _will_ send his workers!

Talking With God

Have the leaders gather in groups of three or four to pray together about the need for more volunteers in their area of children's ministry. Have a volunteer in each group lead in the following "seasons of prayer."

Step 1: Spring—Planting the Seeds

● Read aloud Ephesians 4:11: **"It was he who gave some to be apostles, some to be prophets, some to be evangelists, and some to be pastors and teachers."**

● Say: **God knows those he is gifting and calling to work with our kids. Let's pray that those he is touching will recognize the call and respond to it.**

LEADER TIP:

Rather than read a Scripture yourself, ask for a volunteer to look up the verse and read it aloud to the group.

Allow two or three minutes for the groups to pray together quietly.

 ● Say: <u>God is the Lord of the harvest. We need to ask him, and he</u> <u>*will* send his workers!</u>

Step 2: Summer—Caring for the Plants

● Read aloud 1 Thessalonians 5:16-18: **"Be joyful always; pray continually; give thanks in all circumstances, for this is God's will for you in Christ Jesus."**

● Say: **Now let's offer prayers of thanksgiving for all that God is doing and will do in our ministry and for the workers we know he will be sending.** Allow two or three minutes for the groups to pray together quietly.

 ● Say: <u>God is the Lord of the harvest. We need to ask him, and he</u> <u>*will* send his workers!</u>

Step 3: Fall—Harvesting the Crop

● Read aloud Matthew 9:37-38: **"Then he said to his disciples, 'The harvest is plentiful but the workers are few. Ask the Lord of the harvest, therefore, to send out workers into his harvest field.'"**

● Say: **We need to rest in the confidence that sending new volunteers is, ultimately, God's responsibility. Now let's spend time in prayer asking him to send workers to meet some of our specific needs.** Allow two or three minutes for the groups to pray together quietly.

 ● Say: <u>God is the Lord of the harvest. We need to ask him, and he</u> <u>*will* send his workers!</u>

A Biblical Challenge

Pass out copies of 1 Thessalonians 5:24 to all the participants. Invite them to read the verse out loud with you: **"The one who calls you is faithful and he will do it."**

Say: **I'd like everyone to memorize this Scripture during the next week. It promises us that God will be faithful in working out all the details of our spiritual growth. And for us as ministry leaders, that includes giving us faith to believe that he will provide workers for the ministry.**

Let's say the verse again, but we'll change the emphasis each time. I'll say it first, then you repeat after me.

Read: **"The one who calls you is faithful and *he* will do it."** Pause to allow the group to repeat the verse, with the emphasis on "he."

Say: **He is an awesome God. Nothing is too difficult for him!**

Read: **"The one who calls you is faithful and he *will* do it."** Pause to allow the group to repeat the verse, with the emphasis on "will."

Say: **We can depend on God to do what he says he will do.**

Read: **"The one who calls you is faithful and he will *do it.*"** Pause to allow the group to repeat the verse, with the emphasis on "do it."

Say: **Not only will he do it, Ephesians 3:20 says he "is able to do im-measurably more than all we ask or imagine."**

Read with joy: **"The one who calls you is faithful and he will do it."** Pause to allow the group to repeat the whole verse with enthusiasm.

Say: **We can be joyful because we know <u>God is the Lord of the har-vest. We need to ask him, and he <i>will</i> send his workers!</u>**

♥ *In His Footsteps*

Use this devotion at an annual planning meeting with your leaders (or with your whole staff of volunteers) to excite them about the miraculous things God has planned for your ministry. Allow approximately fifteen to twenty minutes.

Words to Encourage People Who Love Kids

God has a wonderful plan for our lives—and our ministry!

The Bible Basis

"In his heart a man plans his course, but the Lord determines his steps" (Proverbs 16:9).

" 'For I know the plans I have for you,' declares the Lord, 'plans to pros-per you and not to harm you, plans to give you hope and a future' " (Jeremiah 29:11).

PREPARE FOR THIS SESSION

● Read and ponder Proverbs 16:9 and Jeremiah 29:11. What plans do you think God has for your life and for the children's ministry at your church?

● Ask your senior pastor to plan to attend the devotion and speak to the chil-dren's ministry team, or have him tape-record or videotape a three- or four-minute message of appreciation and encouragement. Have him include some of the fol-lowing points:

✱ The children's ministry leaders are vital to the future of the ministry at your church. (Explain why.)

✱ Children are not the church of the future—they are the church of today. (They are also the future of the church.)

✶ The children's staff doesn't often get recognized for all of its work, but God notices what each worker does in the children's ministry every Sunday!

Ask him to close his message by saying: "God has a wonderful plan for our lives—and our ministry!"

● Gather your supplies: pens, scissors, and one or two sheets of construction paper (various colors) for each person attending; three clear jars; a bag of walnuts (or other large nuts) with shells; and a bag of sand.

● Fill one jar with walnuts. Pour enough sand over the nuts to fill the jar to the top, making sure all the nooks and crannies around the nuts are filled. This is the number of walnuts and the amount of sand you will need. Now dump out the mixture, and separate the nuts from the sand. Put the nuts in one jar and the sand in another.

● Tell your team in advance that you will be meeting in a certain room in the church, but actually arrange for the meeting to be held in a different room. On a note on the door of the first room, write: "Our plans have changed. Follow the footsteps to our meeting room."

● Cut out a number of construction paper footprints and mark a trail from the sign to the new meeting room. Have fun with the path by going through other classrooms or around buildings.

● Snack and decorating tips: Line shoe boxes with brightly colored napkins, and fill them with popcorn and pretzels.

A Biblical Challenge

Arrive early, and wait in the meeting room while your leaders wind their way through the church, following the footprints to the correct door. Meet them with a greeting.

Say: **Welcome! Did you have any trouble finding the room?**

Once everyone has arrived and is seated, open your time together by asking them to share their answers to the following questions:

● **How did you feel when you arrived at the first door and found out you had to follow the footsteps to find our meeting?**

● **How is this like or unlike having to trust God's leading in our lives and ministries?**

Read aloud Proverbs 16:9. Say: **Think about one time in your life when you came to a closed door, and you found that God had a different path for you to take. Now turn to the person next to you** (a person who does not have a partner can form a group of three), **and share with one another the answers to these questions:**

● **How did God lead you in a different way than you planned or expected?**

● **How did God's plan turn out?**

Give three or four minutes for the partners to share.

Read aloud Jeremiah 29:11. Ask:

- Is it easier for you to make your own plans or to seek God for *his* plans?
- Why are God's plans for us better than our own?

Say: <u>God has a wonderful plan for our lives—and our ministry!</u>

Setting Priorities

Pull out the three jars—one with nuts, one with sand, and one empty.

Say: **Although we know that our work with children is important, sometimes our busy lives just don't seem to allow for the most important things to get done!**

As you speak, slowly pour the sand into the empty jar until it is half full. Say: **This sand represents the "urgencies" of life that take up our time and energy but aren't always what we would really consider most important to us. They are things like laundry, paying bills, cooking, and shuttling kids to activities. Even good church responsibilities can take up our time—things like serving on committees, cleaning up classrooms, you name it!**

Display the jar of walnuts. Say: **Of course, all of us would like to be able to spend all of our time on the things we consider most important. These walnuts represent the important things** (drop a walnut into the jar half full of sand each time you mention an item)—**things like family time, our marriages, our prayer life, Bible study, preparing for Sunday school, teaching kids, quality friendships...** Continue until the jar is filled; there will be walnuts left over.

Say: **If our priorities aren't straight, we simply won't be able to fit everything into our lives!**

Remove the walnuts, then put both the nuts and the sand back into their original containers. Then start to refill the empty jar, this time with the nuts first.

Say: **We must focus our energies on the important things first—family time, our marriages, our prayer life, Bible study, our ministry to kids, quality friendships...**

After all the nuts are in the jar, pour the sand in on top to show how it all fits. (Shake the jar if necessary to get the sand to fall into all the nooks and crannies.)

Say: **Our priorities need to be what God wants. After all, <u>God has a</u>**  **<u>wonderful plan for our lives—and our ministry!</u>**

Prayer of Celebration

Say: **Now it's time to think and pray about God's plan for our ministry to kids. But first, our senior pastor has some important thoughts to share with us.**

Ask the pastor to speak at this point, or play the audio or videotape.

When the pastor is done, pray: **God, we thank you for church leaders who** love kids and who share our excitement about ministering to the children in our church. We know you have a plan for our lives and for our ministry. Now we ask that you show us the steps you want us to take. In Jesus' name, amen.

Give each person one or two pieces of construction paper, a pen, and scissors. Have them turn again to the partners they had earlier in the devotion. Direct the partners to take turns standing on the construction paper and tracing around one another's shoes. (Two small or average adult shoes will fit on one piece of paper— but some shoes will need two sheets!) Afterward, have them cut out the footprints.

Say: **Think about the future of our ministry together and imagine what the children's ministry at our church could look like in one year... five years...ten years. Now write down one of your dreams on each of your footprints.**

Have several people share what they wrote with the whole group. Say: **It's exciting to know that God has all of our dreams in his hands. God can take our different visions and work them together into one wonderful plan.**

Lead the group in a time of spontaneous prayer, celebrating the awesome vision for ministry God has planted in each person and in the group as a whole. Ask God to reveal his steps for your lives individually and for your ministry together.

Close by praying: **Thank you, God, that you have a wonderful plan for our lives—and our ministry!** Amen.

Long-Range Planning

After your time of prayer, use the "footprint dreams" to launch into a session of long-range planning.

♥ The Joy of the Lord Is Our Strength

Use this devotion at a gathering of your leaders and volunteers to challenge them to lean upon God's strength, especially in tough times. Allow approximately fifteen minutes.

Words to Encourage People Who Love Kids

The joy of the Lord is your strength!

The Bible Basis

"The joy of the Lord is your strength" (Nehemiah 8:10).

PREPARE FOR THIS SESSION

● Read Nehemiah 8:10 and consider its implications for your own life and ministry.

● Gather your supplies: one pushpin and one latex surgical glove for each participant, and permanent markers of various colors. (Optional: a recording of the classic hymn "It Is Well With My Soul" by Horatio G. Spafford.)

● Prepare to sing "The Joy of the Lord" from *Group's Praise and Worship Songbook*.

● Decorate your meeting place with brightly colored balloons and crepe paper. For a snack, serve miniature Almond Joy candy bars.

Stories of Real Joy

Ask: **How many of you would like to have more joy in your life?** Watch for a show of hands. (It should include just about everyone!)

Say: **When we hear the word "joy," we think of many things. Happy feelings. Excited emotions. Bliss. But joy is not just a feeling. It's not a mere emotion that denies the sometimes harsh realities of our lives. It's not a mood that we can put on and take off.**

The Bible says joy is our very strength.

Read aloud Nehemiah 8:10. Say: **Listen while I tell you about someone who knew true joy.**

Share one or both of the following stories, depending on the time you have available:

● **The Story of Lila Trotman** (From *Daws: The Story of Dawson Trotman* by Betty Skinner)

Read: **Lila Trotman knew joy. Her husband, Dawson Trotman, was the founder and president of the Navigators. In this capacity, he revived the principle of discipleship and built this concept back into the modern church. "Daws," as his friends called him, was responsible for bringing hundreds of people to the Lord and for creating a worldwide ministry** dedicated to spreading the gospel and discipling men, women, and children. But most of all, he was a devoted husband and father.

One day during a conference Lila and her husband were attending, a friend and partner in the ministry, Jack Wyrtzen, took Daws water-skiing on the lake. After a couple of laps by themselves, the two men swung back near the shore to pick up other conference participants for a ride. Dawson asked a lifeguard to get Lila so she could join them. The lifeguard was unable to find her, however, so the boat loaded up with new riders and took off again.

While they were cutting across the wakes and waves on the lake, Daws asked two of the girls in the boat if they could swim. One could not. Just then a crash on a wave tossed Daws and the non-swimmer out of the boat.

Although he was able to hold on to the girl's hand in the cold water until help came for her, Dawson Trotman was soon too exhausted to save himself. It had taken all of his strength to hold the girl up. Ultimately, the other swimmers were unable to save this fifty-year-old man who had loved life and loved God.

While others were shocked and grieving, Lila Trotman, his widow, insisted that the conference go on. Her peace and joy at the conference's evening meeting—a mere four hours later—trumpeted her outstanding faith.

"God prepared my heart for the news I received today," she said in a calm, steady voice. "Heaven gets richer all the time, and it's richer tonight. Praise God for almost twenty-four of the most blessed years of my life with this man of God."

Say: Lila Trotman knew that the joy of the Lord was her strength. The joy of the Lord is *your* strength, too!

● **The Story of Horatio G. Spafford** (From *101 Hymn Stories* by Kenneth W. Osbeck)

Read: Horatio G. Spafford knew joy. Spafford was a layman in a Presbyterian church in Chicago. Besides being a successful lawyer, he was active in the ministries of several key leaders of his day, including D.L. Moody. He was respected for his devout Christian walk at church and in the community.

Spafford wanted to join Moody in one of his evangelistic crusades in Great Britain. He also wanted to give his wife and four daughters a needed vacation. So he decided to do both and booked a trip for his entire family to Europe in November 1873.

At the last minute, however, Spafford's business kept him from making the trip with his family. He expected to join his wife and daughters a few days later when he sent them ahead on the S.S. Ville du Havre.

Tragically, another vessel struck the passenger ship on its way across the Atlantic. The Ville du Havre sank in twelve minutes, and more than two hundred passengers died.

Several days later the survivors arrived in Wales. Spafford's wife sent a wire to her husband in Chicago: "Saved alone." Spafford left as soon as possible to cross the Atlantic and join his wife.

It is believed that Horatio Spafford was somewhere near the site where his four daughters drowned when he penned the words to the classic hymn "It Is Well With My Soul." Play a recording of the hymn (people can sing along if they know it) or read the following words aloud:

"When peace, like a river, attendeth my way,
When sorrows like sea billows roll–
Whatever my lot, Thou hast taught me to say,
It is well, it is well with my soul.
Tho Satan should buffet, tho trials should come,
Let this blest assurance control,
That Christ hath regarded my helpless estate
And hath shed His own blood for my soul."

Say: Horatio G. Spafford knew that the joy of the Lord was his strength. The joy of the Lord is your strength, too!

A Biblical Challenge

Ask:

● After hearing this story [or stories], how would you define "biblical joy"?

● How is that different from the way most of the world thinks of joy? (It isn't based on circumstances. It doesn't depend on feelings.)

Say: Real joy—the biblical kind—is that unshakable confidence that God has your life in the palm of his hand and is watching over every detail. There are two keys: realizing that God is totally in control and knowing that he is perfect in every way.

Read aloud Psalm 115:3: "Our God is in heaven; he does whatever pleases him," and Proverbs 17:22: "A joyful heart is good medicine, but a broken spirit dries up the bones" (New American Standard Bible).

Say: We're going to practice the medicinal benefits of joy—remembering that God is in heaven, holding all of our concerns and every detail of our lives in his hands.

Give each person a latex glove. Have participants blow up the gloves and tie off the cuff ends. Pass out permanent markers and ask each person to write on the glove, in one or two-word phrases, some of the specific worries, problems, or burdens in life.

Have everyone remain quiet while they do this, and play some quiet music in the background (perhaps "It Is Well With My Soul," if the recording is available to you).

Thank You, God

Lead your workers in a responsive prayer time.

Say: **Think about those things that you wrote on your gloves as we pray together responsively. Every time I say, "Thank you, God," you say,** **"The joy of the Lord is our strength!"**

For all the ways that you look out for us and our ministry, we thank you, God... (The joy of the Lord is our strength!)

For all the ways that you love us even when we don't deserve it, we thank you, God... (The joy of the Lord is our strength!)

For giving us strength when we trust in you, even in the tough times, we thank you, God... (The joy of the Lord is our strength!)

Amen!

LEADER TIP:

When singing is part of your devotional, consider printing the words on a chalkboard or dry-erase board or using an overhead projector to make it easier for everyone to join in.

A Musical Encouragement

Lead participants in singing "The Joy of the Lord" while they hold their inflated gloves.

For the second and third verses, substitute these words: "If you want joy in ministry, then trust in God," and "When I bring my cares to him, he gives me joy!"

At the end of the song, have everyone pop their gloves with pushpins to praise the God who carries our burdens.

Lead the group in a cheer and shout: **The joy of the Lord is our strength!**

DeVⱷTiⱷNS FⱷR teaCHeRS aND HeLPeRS

♥ *Never Give Up*

Use this devotion to challenge your teachers and helpers to be "marathon ministers"—to go the distance in ministry and experience the blessings of long-term commitment. (It's perfect for a staff meeting when it is time for volunteers to commit to a new term of service!) Allow approximately twenty minutes.

Words to Encourage People Who Love Kids

Never give up! You will reap a harvest!

┌─The Bible Basis────────

"Let us not become weary in doing good, for at the proper time we will reap a harvest if we do not give up" (Galatians 6:9).

PREPARE FOR THIS SESSION

● Read Galatians 6:9, and consider its implications for your own ministry.

● Gather your supplies: one one-hundred-piece jigsaw puzzle for every five or six participants and prizes (a candy bar or other small gift) for every participant you expect to attend.

● Make "challenge cards" on slips of paper or index cards. Make one challenge card for every five or six people, making sure each challenge is used at least once. Fold the cards in half with these words on the inside:

✶ Challenge 1—Build a bridge from one chair (or table) to another using only your bodies.

✶ Challenge 2—Carry something twenty-seven times your size (about the size of an airplane).

✶ Challenge 3—Have two people fight. Cut one person's head off and have this person keep fighting.

● To decorate your room, cover tables with red and white checkered table-cloths. Spread plastic ants on the tables. (You can find these in novelty stores.) Decorate your walls with large cutouts of ants carrying crumbs and twigs.

● Serve ants-on-a-log (celery with peanut butter and raisins) for your snack. For each snack plate, make a flag by gluing a small piece of paper to a toothpick and sticking it in one of the celery pieces. Have the flag read: "Ants never give up!"

It Pays to Not Give Up

Spread the puzzles out on separate tables ahead of time. As the participants arrive, say: **You may start assembling the puzzles in teams of five or six.**

You will have until (state a time about five minutes after your meeting's official "start" time) **to put the puzzle together. At that time, I will hand out prizes!**

Every minute or so, remind everyone that time is almost up. After five minutes have passed, award prizes to each person who continued working on the puzzle the whole time.

Say: **You may have expected the prizes to go to the team that got the furthest on its puzzle. You even may have been discouraged by thinking your team wasn't accomplishing enough to win a prize. But these prizes go to any of you who have continued working without giving up!**

With everyone still in their puzzle groups, ask:

● **How did you feel being asked to put together the puzzle in such a short amount of time?**

● **How was this experience like or unlike trying to live the Christian life?**

● **How was this like or unlike teaching children to live for God?**

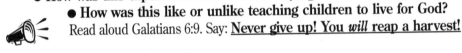 Read aloud Galatians 6:9. Say: **Never give up! You _will_ reap a harvest!**

A Powerful Man's Words of Wisdom

Say: **I want to share a story with you about Winston Churchill, the famous British prime minister.**

Read: **During World War II, Britain experienced some truly dark and dreadful days. More than once Churchill seemed to look defeat straight in the eye—especially as the rest of Europe fell to the Germans. But he led his country—and the Allied forces—to victory.**

Churchill knew how to endure. He worked fourteen-hour days, keeping six secretaries busy, until he retired at age eighty-one. Even then he didn't give up his seat in the House of Commons until his death at the age of ninety. No wonder his grandmother coined his nickname, "Bulldog."

After the war, Churchill was asked to deliver the commencement speech at Oxford University's graduation. The crowd anticipated a lengthy speech with great words of wisdom from this giant of a man who had

helped save the world.

When Churchill's time on the podium finally arrived, his host introduced him by noting his impressive list of accomplishments and honors. Churchill stood and waited for the thunderous applause to die down before he began to speak.

The graduates sat on the edge of their chairs, waiting for the profound words of such a legendary figure. Churchill cleared his throat.

"Never give up! Never, never give up! Never, never, never give up!" he said. And then he sat down.

The audience was stunned—then awed. After all, if Winston Churchill had given up, all of Europe would have fallen to the Nazis.

Many years have passed since this address, and still Churchill's brief words deliver far more impact than many lengthier addresses. What a pointed message—one that was truly lived by the messenger!

Say: <u>Never give up! You *will* reap a harvest!</u>

Ant Power

With participants still in groups of five or six, say: **I'm going to give each group a challenge card containing a physical challenge for the group to accomplish. I will give you two minutes to prepare to meet the challenge, then you'll take turns showing the whole group what you are able to do. Don't open your cards until I tell you to do so.**

Pass out one challenge card to each group. (If you have more than three groups, repeat one or more of the challenges. If you have only a few participants, let them try all three challenges.)

After all of the groups have their cards, say: **You may read your challenge cards.** For a moment, turn a deaf ear to the moaning and complaining you will hear!

Then say: **What? Are you giving up already? Oh, I guess I forgot to tell you that I want you to pretend to be a group of ants and act out what is written on your card. You still have two minutes to prepare.**

After two minutes, ask for each group to act out their challenge. Give these interesting "ant facts" after each demonstration:

● Challenge 1—Say: **Ants are creative! Army ants in South America can build bridges to get wherever they need to go by holding on to one another's bodies. No matter how big the challenge, ants never give up!**

● Challenge 2—Say: **Ants are determined! An ant will carry home a dead moth twenty-seven times its own size. To complicate things, the moth often will have to be dragged through the grass or around obstacles. This would be the same as a person carrying an airplane through a forest. Ants never give up!**

● Challenge 3—Say: **Ants are tough! When an ant gets into a fight, its**

Devotions for Teachers and Helpers 23

head and abdomen can keep on fighting even if the head is severed. Each segment of the body will go on biting, kicking, and fighting until death. No challenge causes an ant to stop. Ants never give up!

As teachers and helpers in the children's ministry, we need to be creative, determined, and tough—willing and able to hang in there for the long haul. <u>Never give up! You *will* reap a harvest!</u>

A Biblical Challenge

Read aloud Galatians 6:9. Say: **Think back to the puzzle activity we started out with and how you felt during that experience. I know many of you felt anxious or frustrated, and you would have liked to forget about the whole thing. Now think about one aspect of your life or ministry which makes you feel frustrated, anxious, or defeated. Turn to a partner and share the frustration you are thinking about.** (If someone cannot find a partner, have that person join another team to make a threesome.)

Give everyone a minute to share with their partners. Then ask them to tell one another their answers to these questions:

● **How is God using this frustration to teach you endurance?**

● **If you stick with it, what might be the coming harvest that God will give?**

Say: **Now take a moment to pray silently for your partner's endurance in that area.**

Close the prayer time by saying: **Lord, we believe we will reap a harvest if we don't give up. For the sake of the children and for the sake of your kingdom, help us to endure with joy and grace. Amen.**

Say: <u>Never give up! You *will* reap a harvest!</u>

♥ *Investing in a Future Harvest*

Use this devotion at a meeting of all your teachers and helpers, including the "behind-the-scenes" heroes, to show just how much God appreciates everything your volunteers do for the kids of his harvest field. Allow approximately ten minutes, with a snack time afterward.

Words to Encourage People Who Love Kids

Regardless of your role in ministry, you get to enjoy the harvest!

PREPARE FOR THIS SESSION

● Read John 4:35b-37, and consider its implications for the different kinds of volunteers who work in the children's ministry.

● Gather your supplies: a small cup of candy corn for each group of four or five participants, a strip of sod or green felt cut into squares (optional), one six- to eight-inch red clay pot for every four to six participants, chocolate ice cream, chocolate cookies or wafers, cardboard (for use with optional sod), plastic flowers, serving spoons, plastic bowls and spoons, and a bouquet of fresh flowers.

● Prepare "flower pot" ice cream snacks: Run the clay pots through the dishwasher to clean them. Fill the pots with chocolate ice cream, and crumble chocolate cookies or wafers over the top. Place the filled pots in the freezer for a day or two before the meeting.

● If you're using sod, place each square of sod on cardboard.

● Just before the meeting, remove the flower pot snacks from the freezer. Place a square of sod or green felt on each meeting table as a base for your snack pots. Stick plastic flowers in the pots for color.

The Journey of the Flowers

Bring a bouquet of fresh flowers to the staff meeting, and set them on a front table. Say: **Aren't these flowers beautiful?**

Invite participants to pass them around and smell them. Say: **You know, it took a lot of people to get these flowers here to us today so that we could enjoy them. Before they were harvested,**

● **someone tilled the fields;**

● **someone else planted the seeds;**

● **someone had to make sure they were regularly watered;**

● **other people sprayed for bugs and pulled weeds;**

● **somewhere along the line someone finally harvested them;**

● **someone else took them to the marketplace;**

● **and finally the florist bought them and arranged them so I could bring them to this meeting for all of us to enjoy.**

None of these people are getting to enjoy the fruit of their labor firsthand as we are now—and as *you* will be for the next week! Hand the flowers to one of your volunteers to take home. Choose someone who is new to the children's ministry or who has had a recent birthday or other special event.

Say: **It's different in the kingdom of God. Everyone who has a part in the crop gets to share in the joy of the harvest. Maybe you think your role in bringing kids to the Lord is small or insignificant. But this is a collaborative effort, and we all get to enjoy the fruit. <u>Regardless of your role</u>** **<u>in ministry, you get to enjoy the harvest!</u>**

A Biblical Challenge

Have participants sit in groups of four or five—if possible, according to ministry teams or classroom groups so people in each group have worked together and know one another.

Read aloud John 4:35b-37. Say: **We're going to take a moment to affirm and encourage one another as we recognize the different contributions each of us makes to the process of harvesting the lives of our children.**

Hand a cup of candy corn to one person in each group.

Say: **I'd like the person holding the cup of candy corn to start. Tell the rest of the group how the person on your right assists in harvesting spiritual fruit in children. For example, you might say: "Mary, because you are so cheerful when you greet and register children at the door, you prepare them to be receptive to the teaching that day and you encourage parents to get more involved."**

After you have affirmed the person on your right, you get to eat a piece of candy and pass the cup to that person. That person will then do the same thing with the person on his or her right, and so on until everyone in your group has had a piece and "enjoyed the harvest!"

After everyone has been affirmed, say: **<u>Regardless of your role in ministry, you get to enjoy the harvest!</u>**

A Big Thank You

Say: **I want to read you a letter that might reflect the thoughts of someone who was in your Sunday school class:**

"Hi! I'm graduating from high school this year. As I look back I realize that a lot of people played a significant part in my life while I was growing up. I want to thank these people—and you're one of them!

"Oh, you may not remember me. I was one of your kids in Sunday school ten years ago. My dad was very sick when I started coming. I think his illness made him and Mom decide to start going to church.

"Because my dad died a few months later, my mom had to go back to work and we moved out of town. So I was really only in your class for a few months. But I wanted to write and tell you how often I think about you.

"While Mom was so busy taking care of Dad and then trying to get a new job, you were one of the few adults who made time to listen to me. You really cared. When I was sad, you understood. Sometimes you just sat with me, and we didn't say anything at all.

"I wasn't there long, but you had enough time to tell me the good news about Jesus. I remembered what you said, and a few years later I became a Christian (and so did my mom)!

"Your love and caring, and the excitement you always showed when you were telling us about God, made it easy for me to gain my own faith later on. Although you were miles and years away, I felt as if you were with me that day when I became a Christian. Thanks for taking the time to care."

Say: You see, <u>regardless of your role in ministry, you get to enjoy the harvest!</u>

Talking With the Lord of the Harvest

Say: I'm going to lead us in prayer. After I say each line, take a moment to pray silently to the Lord of the harvest.

Say each line; then pause for silent prayer:

● Think about those adults who were significant in your life as you grew up or when you came to know the Lord. Thank God for the laborers who invested in your life...and for those who harvested you.

● Think about those children who've been in your classroom in the past. Pray for them and for the people who continue to work in their lives.

● Think about the children you have in your classroom right now. Pray for them, and pray that you will someday have the joy of seeing a bountiful harvest from this fresh crop!

After a pause, say: Amen.

Sharing in the Harvest

Pull the artificial flowers out of one of the flower pot snacks, and say: Surprise! All of us really do get to enjoy the harvest! Even though someone else planted these flowers, we all get to eat the ice cream inside the pots. Enjoy!

Hand out serving spoons and plastic bowls and spoons, and let everyone serve themselves from the pots.

Say: Remember, <u>regardless of your role in ministry, you get to enjoy the harvest!</u>

♥ He's the Reason for the Season

Use this devotion to remind your teachers that "God is with us" all the time—and to challenge them to joyfully present a living Jesus in their homes and classrooms throughout the hustle and bustle of the Christmas season. It's perfect to kick off a staff decorating party or Christmas planning meeting. Allow approximately ten to fifteen minutes.

Words to Encourage People Who Love Kids

God is with us—all the time!

The Bible Basis

"All this took place to fulfill what the Lord had said through the prophet: 'The virgin will be with child and will give birth to a son, and they will call him Immanuel'—which means, 'God with us' " (Matthew 1:22-23).

PREPARE FOR THIS SESSION

● Read Matthew 1:22-23. Think about what "Immanuel" means to you in your life and ministry.

● Gather your supplies: a tape recorder or CD player, a sound-effects recording of a thunderstorm (available at nature specialty shops), a blanket for each participant (you might ask them to bring their own), and a flashlight.

● Make Bible verse cards. Look up and write the following verses on index cards:

✔ **Deuteronomy 20:1b, 4:** "Do not be afraid of them, because the Lord your God, who brought you up out of Egypt, will be with you...For the Lord your God is the one who goes with you to fight for you against your enemies to give you victory."

✔ **Deuteronomy 31:6:** "Be strong and courageous. Do not be afraid or terrified because of them, for the Lord your God goes with you; he will never leave you nor forsake you."

✔ **Matthew 28:20b:** "And surely I am with you always, to the very end of the age."

✔ **Hebrews 13:5-6:** "Keep your lives free from the love of money and be content with what you have, because God has said, 'Never will I leave you; never will I forsake you.' So we say with confidence, 'The Lord is my helper; I will not be afraid. What can man do to me?' "

✔ **1 Peter 5:10:** "And the God of all grace, who called you to his eternal glory in Christ, after you have suffered a little while, will himself restore you and make you strong, firm and steadfast."

● Decorate your room using traditional Christmas items.

● Ask one or more parents to bless the teachers by making homemade Christmas cookies and hot apple cider for a snack.

Everyone Needs Comfort

Give each participant a blanket, or have them hold the ones they brought with them. Say: **To start our time together, I want you to wrap up in your blanket and pretend that you are a small child alone in bed at night.**

Turn out the classroom lights and play sounds from a thunderstorm in the background.

Say: **Think about a time from your childhood when you were frightened, and a parent came to be with you and comfort you. Or think about a time when you comforted a child who was afraid.**

Allow for one or two minutes of quiet thought while the "thunderstorm" continues. Then ask: **Would someone share your story with all of us?** Have three or four volunteers tell about their experiences.

Say: **As kids, there are many times when we need someone to be with us so that we're not afraid. As adults, we also need that comfort at times. It's comforting to know that no matter where we are, <u>God is with us—all the time!</u>**

The Promises of God

Pass out the Bible verse cards to volunteers who are willing to read the verses aloud. Keep the room darkened as much as possible, and pass a flashlight to the volunteers when it is their turn to read.

Turn the lights on, and ask participants to turn to a partner (if someone doesn't have a partner, that person can join one of the pairs). Have them share with their partners the answers to these questions:

● **How was being in the dark room like or unlike living in the world today?** (It can be scary; we're sometimes "in the dark" about how to live our lives; we need the light of Jesus to see things clearly.)

● **How did it feel to hear so many promises that God is with us?**

● **What keeps us from remembering that God is with us?**

A Biblical Challenge

Read aloud Matthew 1:22-23. Say: **In New Testament times, Jesus was born and was physically present with the people for about thirty-three years. He really was *with* them—in the flesh!**

Ask participants to turn to their partners again and share their answers to these questions:

● **What would your reaction be if Jesus said he was coming to live with you for a while?** (I would change a thing or two; I would be very happy; I would be frightened.)

● **How is that like or unlike the way we live our lives today, now that Jesus is not physically present?** (We forget that he is with us all the time; we live as if he is not with us.)

   ● **If you could always keep in mind that God is with you, what areas of your life or ministry would change?**

Say: **The Bible promises: <u>God is with us—all the time!</u>**

Talking With the God Who Is With Us

Say: **Let's take a moment to pray to the God who is with us. We can speak one-sentence prayers, thanking God for sending his Son to earth to save us and for his faithfulness in always being with us.**

Ask one of your lead teachers to start, and allow people to speak up in prayer as they feel led to do so. Close the prayer time by saying: **<u>Thank you, God, that you are with us—all the time.</u> Amen.**

♥ *Stars in God's Galaxy*

Use this devotion at a planning or training meeting to help your teachers feel like "stars" and to revitalize their trust in God for the results of their ministries. Allow approximately fifteen minutes.

Words to Encourage People Who Love Kids

Have faith in God! He's got the whole world in his hands...including your ministry to the kids.

> *"Now faith is being sure of what we hope for and certain of what we do not see. This is what the ancients were commended for"* (Hebrews 11:1-2).

PREPARE FOR THIS SESSION

● Read Hebrews 11:1-2. Think about the role faith plays in your life and in the children's ministry at your church.

● Gather your supplies: a candle and holder; matches; a glass jar big enough to cover the candle; a mini-marshmallow; a toothpick; a can of aerosol hair spray; a flip chart, chalkboard, or dry-erase board, with chalk or markers; enough markers or pens for every participant to have one.

● Cut out a large yellow construction paper star for each of your current teachers and helpers—whether or not they will be at the meeting. Attach a photograph of each worker to a star, and write his or her name below the picture. (If you don't have photographs, leave enough space on each star for a picture; then ask participants to bring photos of themselves to the meeting. Or use an instant-print camera and take the photos on the spot.)

Add statistical categories (like those on baseball cards) below the name on each star. The "stats" can include the teacher or leader's room number, grade or age of kids, number of years in service, or even a favorite Bible verse.

● Prepare to sing "I Believe in Jesus" from *The Group Songbook* and "He's Got the Whole World in His Hands" from *Group's Singable Songs for Children's Ministry.*

● For decoration, hang a piece of newsprint across the wall, and label it: "[your church name] Children's Ministry Hall of Faith." Attach the yellow stars. Leave space below each star for additional comments. In addition, hang large rubber balls from the ceiling with string to represent the sun and Earth and other planets.

● For a snack, serve "Galaxy Sundaes" using vanilla ice cream, chopped-up Mars candy bars, "spacey" sprinkles, marshmallow "moon" creme, and "out-of-this-world" hot fudge! If you really want this time to be remembered, serve the sundaes *flambé* by soaking a sugar cube in vanilla or almond extract, placing it on top of the sundae, and lighting it!

The Master of the Universe

Say: **Our God is awesome. He does so much more to uphold our lives and our world than we even know. Think about how these facts of science affect us. Remember that it is God who is responsible for them on a daily basis.**

● Light a candle. Then say: **The earth's temperature is controlled by the sun, which is the perfect distance away from earth (93 million miles) and** the perfect temperature to sustain life on earth (twelve thousand degrees Fahrenheit).

Allow several people to test this concept by holding their hands near the flame. Have them experience how it feels good to have their hands just the right distance from the candle; if their hands are too close, the heat is too intense, but they can't feel the warmth if their hands are too far away.

● Put a mini-marshmallow on a toothpick and hold it by the candle's flame. Rotate it to brown it without burning. Say: **The earth rotates on its axis 365 times each year, which allows for days and nights that are in sync with our bodies and allows for the proper heating and cooling of the earth and all its life forms.**

● Say: **The air we breathe is 21 percent oxygen, just right for human beings. If it had too much oxygen, the air would explode.**

Hold up the can of hair spray and say: **If I were to spray this into the candle, the flame would ignite the spray.** (To play it safe, don't spray the flame!)

Say: **The balance of the chemicals around our planet is extremely important to our survival. Too little oxygen would cause death by suffocation.** Place a jar over the candle until the flame is extinguished.

Say: **Whether we believe in God or not, we benefit from the work he does in our universe. <u>Have faith in God! He's got the whole world in his hands...including your ministry to the kids!</u>**

Lead the group in singing "He's Got the Whole World in His Hands."

The Faith Requirement

Say: **We rely on God for the air we breathe, for the proper rotation of the earth, for the right amount of heat from the sun, and for so many other things. Can you add to the list? What else do we need to rely on God for in our lives?** As participants offer their insights, list their answers on the board or flip chart.

If no one else brings it up, say: **As teachers, we can work really hard at preparing and teaching our lessons, but we must ultimately trust God for the spiritual birth and growth of our kids. And that requires faith.**

Say: **<u>Have faith in God! He's got the whole world in his hands...including your ministry to the kids.</u>**

A Biblical Challenge

Read aloud Hebrews 11:1-2; then have the teachers turn to a partner (someone who does not have a partner can join one of the pairs).

Say: **Think of a time in your life when you were in some uncomfortable situation or difficulty and you really didn't know what was going to happen** next or how everything would turn out. You just had to trust God. Tell your partner about that time. Pause a minute or two to allow everyone time to think and share.

Say: **Now share your answers to these questions with your partner:**
- **How did God answer you in that situation?**
- **How did that experience affect the way you trust God today?**

Say: **Have faith in God! He's got the whole world in his hands...including your ministry to the kids.**

Stars in the Hall of Faith

Read aloud Hebrews 11:1-2 again. Say: **If you continue reading in Hebrews 11, you find a long list of people from the past who lived by faith even though they did not see what they were believing in—people like Noah, Abraham and Sarah, Moses, and King David.**

All of you are "stars" in God's "Hall of Faith," too. Point to the banner you have made with the teachers' and helpers' stars on it. Say: **Whenever you teach and help children, you are exercising your faith that God holds the whole world—and your ministry to the kids—in his hands.**

Pass out markers to everyone. Say: **I want each of you to come up, choose someone's star, and write in the space below it one thing you think qualifies that person to be in "[your church name] Children's Ministry Hall of Faith." For example, you might write, "Sarah always prays before class," or "John stands on God's Word." If you don't know the person well, you might just write a challenge or a word of encouragement like, "Trust in the Lord with all your heart."** (If you have a large number of participants, you may want to have them come forward in groups of five or six.)

LEADER TIP:

Be aware of teachers or helpers who are not as well-known as others in your ministry. Be ready to add some comments under their pictures if others do not.

When everyone is done, say: **Have faith in God! He's got the whole world in his hands...including your ministry to the kids.** Then lead your team in the song "I Believe in Jesus."

Talking with God

Have three volunteers look up and read these passages aloud:
- Psalm 139:5,16b: "You hem me in—behind and before; you have laid your hand upon me...All the days ordained for me were written in your book before one of them came to be."
- Isaiah 46:9-10: "Remember the former things, those of long ago; I am God, and there is no other; I am God, and there is none like me. I make known the end

from the beginning, from ancient times, what is still to come. I say: My purpose will stand, and I will do all that I please."

• Daniel 4:35: "All the peoples of the earth are regarded as nothing. He does as he pleases with the powers of heaven and the peoples of the earth. No one can hold back his hand or say to him: 'What have you done?' "

Say: **Let's close our time with one-sentence prayers of praise and thanksgiving. Thank God that he is sovereign and loving and that we can trust God to take care of our universe and our kids.**

Ask a lead teacher to begin the prayer time. When everyone who wants to has prayed, say: **Amen.**

Then address your teachers and say with enthusiasm: **Have faith in God! He's got the whole world in his hands...including your ministry to the kids!**

♥ *My Burden Is Light*

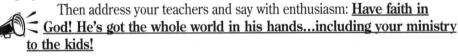

Use this devotion at a meeting of your children's ministry team about halfway through the year or when volunteers seem tired and are mentioning "burnout." Use this time to lighten their loads and help them feel the freedom that comes from walking with God. Allow approximately ten minutes.

Words to Encourage People Who Love Kids

Be free! When you're yoked with God, the burden is light!

─The Bible Basis─

"Come to me, all you who are weary and burdened, and I will give you rest. Take my yoke upon you and learn from me, for I am gentle and humble in heart, and you will find rest for your souls. For my yoke is easy and my burden is light" (Matthew 11:28-30).

PREPARE FOR THIS SESSION

• Read Matthew 11:28-30. Think about your own burdens—whether at home, at work, or in your ministry—and give them to God in prayer.

• Gather your supplies: enough pens or markers for everyone (or for every two or three people to share), two or three spools of clear tape, and a trash can.

- Photocopy the "Life's Burdens" handout (p. 38) for each participant.
- To decorate your room, have someone build a simple yoke for you out of a 5-foot length of wood and two 20-inch lengths of garden hose. Use short nails to attach the two lengths of hose to the wood, creating a yoke similar to the one shown in the "Life's Burdens" drawing on page 38. Place it in the front of the room, and use it as a prop during the devotion time.
- Serve licorice "whips" and chocolate milk (or milkshakes) for your snack, and put small plastic cow figures from a toy or novelty store on the serving trays.

Yoked Together

As your teachers and helpers arrive, hand each one a copy of the "Life's Burdens" handout (p. 38) and a pen or marker.

Say: **While we're waiting to get started, I want you to take this yoke and write on it something that is a burden in your life. Maybe it's your job or a problem with a family member at home or something having to do with your ministry to kids at church. Then use the tape to attach your yoke to the wall somewhere in the room.**

Once everyone has arrived and taped a yoke to the wall, have each person choose a partner. (Someone who does not have a partner can team up with you.) Partners should stand side by side.

Say: **Stretch your arms out and put your hands on your partner's shoulders. Now walk around the room pretending to be a team of oxen that has been yoked together. As you do so, I want the partner on the left to be uncooperative. Try to pull away from your partner as you walk.** Pause for a minute while everyone begins to move around the room.

Say: **Now, instead of trying to pull away, I want that same person to follow your partner's lead. Try working together as you walk around.**

After another minute, ask the twosomes to sit down with another set of partners, forming groups of four (or six at the most). Have everyone share their answers to these questions:

- How did you feel about being yoked together as a team?
- What made this activity hard or easy?

A Biblical Challenge

Hold up the wooden yoke you have made. You may even want to put it on and have a partner wear it with you. Say: **A yoke is sometimes used to teach a younger ox how to pull a load. The older, more experienced ox plods along, keeping the younger ox in line and on track. The older ox never follows the younger one's lead; it's always the younger ox that eventually gets the point!**

In the same way, we are "yoked" with Jesus. He is our trainer. The yoke is used to make the job easier and to train us in life. God does not control us or manipulate us. Rather, he works with us and guides us.

Read aloud Matthew 11:28-30. Say: **Jesus said his yoke is easy and his burden is light. But if we're honest, we have to admit that sometimes the burdens in our lives feel anything but light.**

Have the small groups answer these questions:

● **What do we do to make Jesus' yoke hard and the burden heavy sometimes?** (Fight against the leader, Jesus; refuse to cooperate with his plan for our lives; try to go faster or slower than his plan.)

● **What can we do to make Jesus' yoke easier and the burden lighter?** (Allow Jesus to lead; follow the direction he sets for us; stay with his pace.)

● **How was this experience we've just had—being yoked to one another—like or unlike what happens when we try living the Christian life?**

Say: <u>**Be free! When you're yoked with God, the burden is light!**</u>

A Wise and Loving Father

Read or tell this story, adapted from the June 1997 issue of Homelife magazine: **Corrie ten Boom was the Christian daughter of Casper ten Boom, a Dutch watchmaker who became an underground helper of the Jews during World War II. Corrie was the only member of her family to survive the Nazi death camps.**

A favorite memory of Corrie's during those awful years in the camp was of a train ride with her father forty years earlier. Whenever she replayed this scene in her mind, it reminded her that God was always with her, even in the death and darkness of the concentration camp.

When she was eleven years old, Corrie accompanied her father on the train to Amsterdam so he could set his watch by the clock tower of the Naval Observatory. During the ride, Corrie asked her father a very difficult question. She had read about something in school that she did not understand.

She asked, "Papa, what is sex sin?"

Instead of answering, her father pulled his heavy suitcase down from the overhead rack and set it on the floor.

He asked her, "Corrie, will you carry this off the train?"

She told him she couldn't lift the suitcase—it was too heavy for such a small girl.

"Yes," he said. "And it would be a pretty poor father who would ask his little girl to carry such a load. It's the same way with knowledge, Corrie. Some knowledge is too heavy for children. When you are older and stronger, you can bear it. But for now, you must trust me to carry it for you."

As an eleven-year-old, Corrie was at peace with her father's answer. As a fifty-year-old in the death camps, she was also at peace that her heavenly Father would not ask her to carry burdens that she could not.

Say: <u>Be free! When you're yoked with God, the burden is light!</u>

Talking to the Burden-Bearer

Have the small groups stand and "yoke up" by holding hands in a circle.

Say: **Let's take a moment to pray to our heavenly Father who promises to help us bear our burdens. Each of you can pray for the person across the circle from you, asking God to help that person walk willingly with Jesus. Ask God to make that person's load easier and the burden lighter.**

Direct the person closest to you in each circle to begin; then have the person to the leader's right go next, and so on around the circle.

Close the prayer by saying: **Thank you, God, that you have promised to help us carry life's burdens. Your yoke *is* easy and your burden *is* light, Lord. Help us to always follow your lead in our lives. Amen.**

Say: **Now everyone can go to the wall, find the yoke that you taped there, tear it up, and put it in this trash can.** <u>Be free! When you're yoked with God, the burden is light!</u>

♥ *Empty Eggs*

As Easter nears, use this devotion to challenge your teachers to convey their excitement about Jesus' resurrection—both to the kids they teach and to the people around them. Allow approximately fifteen to twenty minutes.

Words to Encourage People Who Love Kids

He is risen! He is risen indeed!

┌─The Bible Basis─

"The angel said to the women, 'Do not be afraid, for I know that you are looking for Jesus, who was crucified. He is not here; he has risen, just as he said. Come and see the place where he lay. Then go quickly and tell his disciples: "He has risen from the dead and is going ahead of you into Galilee. There you will see him." Now I have told you'" (Matthew 28:5-7).

LiFE'S BURDENS

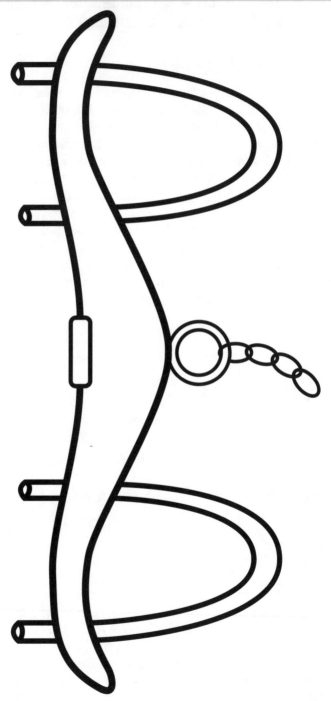

- Read Matthew 28:5-7, and think about what Jesus' resurrection means to you.
- Gather your supplies: For each participant, prepare one piece of crepe paper two to three feet long, a small bag of multi-colored jelly beans, and one copy of the "Jelly Bean Prayer" handout (p. 42).
- Prepare to sing one or more Easter songs from your church hymnal—for example, "Christ the Lord is Risen Today" or "The Easter Song."
- Decorate your room by hanging a cross at the front. Tape to the wall pictures of the Crucifixion, the empty tomb, and the angels greeting the women at the tomb on Easter morning. (Check the visual aides in your children's curriculum for pictures.) Place open, empty plastic eggs on beds of plastic grass on your tables.
- For a snack, prepare "Empty Tombs." Start with several tubes of prepared crescent roll dough (enough for each teacher to have at least two rolls). Into each triangle of dough, place a full-sized marshmallow, and sprinkle with cinnamon sugar. Stretch the dough up and around the marshmallow, pinching it closed on all edges where the dough meets.

Put the rolls on cookie sheets, and bake according to the directions on the package. When they are done, let them cool. The marshmallow will have melted, making a sweet biscuit treat with a hollow center!

LEADER TIP:

If you have access to a kitchen during the meeting, have the teachers make their own "Empty Tombs." Not only are these great to eat warm from the oven, the teachers can transfer the idea to their classrooms and make them for their kids later. Each teacher can prepare one or two triangles. Plan for some discussion or fellowship time while the rolls are baking—or sing some more Easter songs!

The Simplicity of the Good News

Read or tell the following story:

A small country church decided to have a contest one Easter to see which child could make the most beautiful Easter decoration. Each child in the church was given an empty plastic egg and was told to decorate both the outside and the inside of the egg in any way he or she wanted to, thinking of something special about Easter.

One of the children at this church was a little boy named George who had Down syndrome. George asked if he could decorate an egg, too. Everyone wondered what he would do. Although George was never ridiculed, he was, at best, just tolerated. Many people hoped that he would forget about the contest so as not to embarrass himself—or anyone else!

As Easter grew closer, one by one the children began bringing beautifully decorated eggs to church and placing them on a special table that the pastor had reserved at the front of the church. By Easter morning, the table was full of bright, shiny eggs.

The pastor was relieved to see that George's was not among them. He asked the kids who had decorated eggs to come forward and tell the congregation about their eggs and why they chose to decorate them the way they did.

One by one, the kids showed off their elaborate creations, opening the eggs to reveal toy chicks and bunnies, brightly colored grass and other shiny objects. Each explained a special Easter memory or a gift they'd received that inspired their decorations.

After all of the other children had shared, George got up from his seat. With his egg in his hand, he walked up to the pastor. The pastor looked at George and wondered how he would get through the next few awkward moments. He wanted to avoid embarrassing George, so he took the egg from him and quickly set it at the back of the table.

"Open it," George said.

The pastor opened it, and there was nothing inside.

"The tomb is empty," George said, and he quietly walked back to his seat.

Say: The gospel message is simple, isn't it? Although we try to make it more complicated, the good news is really quite plain. We can sum it up this way: He is risen! He is risen indeed!

A Biblical Challenge

Say: Let's say that together. Throughout our session, each time I say the words, "He is risen!" please respond by saying, "He is risen indeed!"

Practice this response a couple of times before going on.

Read aloud Matthew 28:5-7. Say: He is risen! (He is risen indeed!)

Singing His Praises

Give each person a crepe paper streamer. Say: This is your "praise streamer." Let's praise God for the good news of the risen Savior by singing and praising him with our streamers.

Sing one or more Easter songs from your church's hymnal. As you sing, lead your group in waving the streamers left and right, up and down, and in circles.

Say: He is risen! (He is risen indeed!)

Talking With God

Give each teacher a small bag of jelly beans. Say: When I say a color, pick out one jelly bean of that color, eat it, and then pray silently about what this bean represents in the work of Christ.

Using the "Jelly Bean Prayer" (p. 42) as your guide, begin by saying: **Purple. Purple reminds us of our sin. Now silently confess and apologize for the wrong things you've done that made it necessary for Christ to die on the cross. You may eat the jelly beans as you pray.**

Pause long enough for everyone to eat a jelly bean and pray. Then continue in the same fashion with the other colors listed on the handout.

When you're done, give everyone a copy of the "Jelly Bean Prayer." Say: **This may be a good activity for you to use in your classrooms on Easter. It helps tell the good news in a way that kids can experience through their senses.**

After all, they need to know—and we need to remember: He is risen! (He is risen indeed!)

♥ Learning From a Little One

Use this devotion at a training meeting to help teachers get in touch with the fun of being a child and to challenge them to be learners as well as teachers in their classrooms. Allow approximately fifteen minutes.

Words to Encourage People Who Love Kids

Become like a child...a child of God!

The Bible Basis

"He called a little child and had him stand among them. And he said: 'I tell you the truth, unless you change and become like little children, you will never enter the kingdom of heaven. Therefore, whoever humbles himself like this child is the greatest in the kingdom of heaven. And whoever welcomes a little child like this in my name welcomes me' " (Matthew 18:2-5).

PREPARE FOR THIS SESSION

● Read Matthew 18:2-5, and think about what it means to be like a little child.

● Gather your supplies: one Bible, one piece of paper, one pencil, and one pair of children's scissors for each participant.

● Arrange to hold this session in a preschool classroom with smaller tables

Jelly Bean Prayer

 Purple jelly bean:

- Reminds us of our sin.
- Confess and apologize for the wrong things we have done that made it necessary for Christ to die on the cross.

 Red jelly bean:

- Reminds us of the blood Jesus shed.
- Thank Jesus for so freely and lovingly suffering pain and death to pay the price for our souls.

 Orange jelly bean:

- Reminds us of the morning and of the joy of that one special morning when the women found an empty tomb.
- Praise God that Jesus conquered death and rose from the grave on Easter morning!

 White jelly bean:

- Reminds us of God's forgiveness and cleansing from sin.
- Thank God for forgiving you and for separating you from your sin as far as the east is from the west.

 Green jelly bean:

- Reminds us of the new life we have in Christ.
- Thank God for the wonderful new journey on which you accompany him.

 Yellow jelly bean:

- Reminds us of the streets of gold in heaven.
- Praise God that we will be with him in eternity in the home he has gone ahead to prepare for us.

and chairs (or move smaller furniture into your meeting room) to help your teachers "become like little children." Keep some larger chairs handy for people who need them. Have chairs pre-set around the tables to automatically form groups of four or five as everyone arrives and finds a seat.

● Decorate your room by hanging large pictures of children on the walls. Consider investing in pictures of children from around the world that can be used later in a missions education program. Place stuffed animals and children's toys throughout the room.

● For a snack, place bowls of Hershey's Hugs and Kisses chocolate candies on each table, and allow everyone to help themselves. Serve fresh-baked cookies and glasses of ice-cold milk. You might even have a milk-mustache contest!

A Biblical Challenge

Say: **To get started, I'd like everyone to look up Matthew 18:2-5 and read it silently to yourselves.**

After everyone has done this, say: **As you came in, you all sat down in groups of four or five. Now I will give you two to three minutes to decide how your group will silently act out these verses as I read them aloud. You can mime the verses or do whatever you want to do to demonstrate the words.**

After two or three minutes, have two groups at a time come forward—one on your right and one on your left—to act out their scenes while you read the verses. Repeat this until every group has had a turn.

Say: **The Scripture you've just acted out makes an important point. Jesus wants us to** <u>**Become like a child**</u>**...***a child of God!*

Paper Dolls

Give each teacher or helper a piece of paper, a pencil, and a pair of child-sized scissors. Say: **Do you remember making paper doll chains when you were a child? Let's do it now. Fold your paper at least four times accordion-style, then draw a simple outline of half of a doll, with the middle of the doll on one side with the folds and the hand and foot reaching to the other fold. Then cut it out, making sure you don't cut through the fold!**

After teachers and helpers have finished cutting, have them open their chains and appreciate their work. Then have them turn to their partners and discuss their answers to these questions (a person without a partner can join another pair):

● **How did it feel being a little child again—**

> **LEADER TIP:**
> You may need to demonstrate this. Be sure to leave a connection on both sides of the paper where the dolls' hands and feet touch and the body unfolds. Practice cutting dolls before your meeting!

making paper dolls and using small scissors?

● How is this like or unlike what Jesus meant about becoming like a child to enter the kingdom of heaven?

● What qualities have you seen in your students (or your kids at home) that you can incorporate into your life and walk with God?

Say: <u>Become like a child...*a child of God!*</u>

The Student Becomes the Teacher

Say: **One thing that always seems to surprise us as teachers is how much we can learn from our students. Sometimes kids have profound insight into God's Word that we miss if we're not paying attention.**

Read this story:

A church in southern Arizona sent its fifth- and sixth-grade students on a missions trip to Mexico. Thirty kids and six adults spent the day at an orphanage washing lice out of the children's hair, making dinner with flies buzzing everywhere, and continually smelling the raw sewage backed up in the buildings that housed 120 children from birth to 17.

Later, the leaders asked the kids to tell why they thought God had allowed the people in the orphanage to be so poor.

One girl answered: "Maybe we are the ones who are poor because of all we have and that we take it for granted."

There was a long silence as the adults, as much as the kids, tried to process the depth of what this fifth-grader had shared.

Say: **Learning can be a two-way street. Think back to a time when you were a child and you learned something from a teacher. Write what you learned on one side of your paper doll chain.** Pause for a minute as they do this.

Say: **Now think about something you, as an adult, learned from a child. Write that on the other side of your dolls.**

After a minute, ask teachers to turn back to their partners and share their answers to these questions:

● **How did it make you feel to learn something from that teacher? from that child?**

● **Which experience was more humbling to you? Why?**

● **How can we make sure that our children know that we value and welcome their suggestions, opinions, and questions in our classrooms?** (By allowing them to talk; by listening; by incorporating their ideas when possible.)

Say: <u>Become like a child...*a child of God!*</u>

Talking With `Dad'

Say: **We're going to play a game of Simon Says. Simon says, "Stand up."** Everyone should rise.

Say: **Simon says, "Put your hands on your heads." Simon says, "Pray silently for your own faith—not for big theological ideas, but for simple, childlike faith in your own mind."** Give time for everyone to pray.

Say: **Simon says, "Stretch your hands out to your sides." Simon says, "Pray that you can welcome all the children into your classroom, even the ones who may give you trouble sometimes."**

After a moment, say: **Simon says, "Put your hands over your hearts." Simon says, "Pray that God will help you love each child in your classroom unconditionally, just as he loves us."**

After another pause, say: **Simon says, "Kneel," or if that's too uncomfortable, Simon says, "Sit down in your chair." Simon says, "Pray for humility in your life—that you can bow before God and serve his children."** Pause; then say: **Amen.**

♥ The Kids' Kingdom

Use this devotion at a general planning meeting to warm your teachers' hearts, fire their passion for ministering to children, and remind them how close to God's heart children really are. Allow approximately five to ten minutes.

Words to Encourage People Who Love Kids

The kingdom of God belongs to kids!

The Bible Basis

"People were bringing little children to Jesus to have him touch them, but the disciples rebuked them. When Jesus saw this, he was indignant. He said to them, 'Let the little children come to me, and do not hinder them, for the kingdom of God belongs to such as these. I tell you the truth, anyone who will not receive the kingdom of God like a little child will never enter it.' And he took the children in his arms, put his hands on them and blessed them" (Mark 10:13-16).

PREPARE FOR THIS SESSION

● Read Mark 10:13-16, and ask God to give you the kind of love for children that he has.

Don't be intimidated about making your own presentation. Even the most novice photographer can hardly go wrong as long as the subject matter is kids!

● Prepare to sing the familiar song "Jesus Loves the Little Children."

● Make a home video (or a slide show) a couple of Sundays before your meeting. As families come to church, take lots of footage of children's faces. Catch children walking into the church building hand-in-hand with their mom or dad. Tape-record a group of children or a children's choir singing "Jesus Loves Me" to play in the background when you show the video. Near the end of the video, pre-record (or plan to read live) Mark 10:13-16, making sure this portion of the video shows families "bringing little children to Jesus."

● To decorate your room, draw happy faces on a few bouquets of helium-filled balloons. If you're using tables, put large dolls at each table for the centerpieces.

● Serve gingerbread figures or cupcakes for your snack. If time allows, have the teachers decorate their own snacks. Supply frosting and a variety of small candies to decorate the gingerbread figures or to make cupcake faces.

A Biblical Challenge

Say: **Let's pretend for a moment that we are little children. As I read a story to you, I'd like you to follow along and do the motions that I do.**

Read the following story adapted from Mark 10:13-16:

One day, some parents got ready to take their children to see Jesus. "Come on! Let's go!" (Motion to come with your whole arm.)

First, they shuffled through the dusty streets of their city. (Brush your palms away from each other to make a dusty-sounding rhythm.)

When they came to the edge of town, they had to pass through grassy fields. (Rub the tips of your fingers with the thumbs of both hands.)

Soon they came to a hill they had to climb. (Pretend to climb to the top of a hill.)

They could see a crowd of people in the distance. (Shield your eyes and point.)

The adults ran down the hill. (Lean forward and run in place.)

The children rolled down the hill. (Roll your arms in a circle.)

When they reached the crowd, they were out of breath. (Pant.)

Whew! They were finally there! (Wipe your brow.)

They tried to get through the crowd. ("Push" with palms and elbows.)

"Where do you think you're going?" the disciples said. (Repeat the line in a booming voice.)

"To Jesus!" the travelers said. (Repeat the line in a squeaky voice.)

"No, you're not!" (Shake your head.)

"What's happening?" asked Jesus. (Shrug your shoulders to ask a question.)
The travelers said: "We have been on dusty roads (brush your palms together)
And through grassy fields. (Rub your fingertips with both thumbs.)
We've climbed up hills. (Imitate a climbing motion.)
We've rolled down hills. (Roll your forearms in a circle.)
And we've pushed through crowds. (Push with palms and elbows.)
And now that our journey's ended, we'd like to see Jesus, please."
(Clasp your hands together.)
"I am he. (Point to yourself.)
Let the children come to me (beckon with your arms),
Because I love them so." (Hug yourself.)
And the children went to him.

Excerpted from *Wiggly, Giggly Bible Stories About Jesus,* copyright © 1998 Group Publishing, Inc.,
P.O. Box 481, Loveland, CO 80539.

Bringing the Little Children

Show the video footage (or slide show) you have prepared, and play the recording in the background. Afterward, direct the teachers and helpers to form groups of three or four with others who minister in the same age level (for example, nursery, preschool, or elementary).

Ask the small groups to discuss these questions:

● **How would it feel to have Jesus tell you that you kept a child from knowing his love because of something you did?**

● **How do we keep the children from coming to Jesus by some of the things we do or say in Sunday school?** (By boring kids; by being too harsh; by not being excited about the Bible story ourselves.)

● **What can we do differently to make sure that our students know that God loves them?** (Tell them; love them ourselves; make Sunday school the most exciting hour of their week.)

Say: **The kingdom of God belongs to kids!**

Talking to God

Say: **Let's each think about one child in our ministry who really needs to know that God loves him or her. Pray silently for that child, and ask God for wisdom in how we can show God's love.**

After a few minutes, close the prayer by praying: **God, please bless these teachers as they seek to love your children in your name. Amen.**

Jesus Loves the Little Children

Close your devotional by having all of your teachers and helpers sing together "Jesus Loves the Little Children." On the second verse, use these new words:

People were bringing all their children
Just to have him bless their lives.
He said, "Let them come to me!
And do not keep them away
Because the kingdom of God belongs to these."

♥ Love and Forgiveness

Use this devotion at a gathering of your children's ministry team to remind them that Jesus loves them and forgives them just the way they are—and to encourage them to show God's unconditional love to the kids they teach. Allow approximately fifteen minutes.

Words to Encourage People Who Love Kids

Jesus forgives you and loves you—just the way you are!

The Bible Basis

"You are forgiving and good, O Lord, abounding in love to all who call to you" (Psalm 86:5).
"He does not treat us as our sins deserve or repay us according to our iniquities...For he knows how we are formed, he remembers that we are dust" (Psalm 103:10, 14).

PREPARE FOR THIS SESSION

● Read Psalm 86:5 and Psalm 103:10, 14. Consider God's amazing goodness toward you.

● Gather your supplies: one adhesive-strip bandage and one permanent marker for each participant.

● Prepare to sing "Thy Loving Kindness," by Hugh Mitchell, based on Psalm 63:3-4.

● Decorate your room with large red construction paper hearts. Hang or place a large cross in the front of the room to show that Jesus declared his love for us by giving his life for us.

● For a snack, serve heart-shaped cookies that have been broken in half. Provide knives and bowls of frosting so participants can "glue" their heart cookies back together.

Great Expectations

Say: **Think for a moment about the kids who are in your classroom every week. Think of their names, their faces. What are your expectations for each one? Do you expect them to cause trouble? To come up with all the answers? To miss the point?**

You know, our expectations can influence how each child behaves and responds as we teach about the good news of Jesus Christ.

Say: **The story is told of a teacher in the 1960's who was given a roster for one class showing all of the kids' IQ scores. For a second class, the teacher was given a separate roster, but the IQ column had been filled in with the students' locker numbers. The teacher assumed that the locker numbers were the actual IQs of the students!**

At the end of the school year, all of the students' grades were compared. It was discovered that in the first class, the students with higher IQ scores had performed better than those with lower scores. And amazingly, in the second class, the students with higher locker numbers scored significantly better than those with lower locker numbers!

Have participants form groups of two or three. Ask:

● **Are expectations good or bad?** (They can be both!) **Why?**

● **Can you remember a particular time when the expectations of others—parents, teachers, employers, friends—either helped you or hurt you in your life?**

● **What are your expectations for the different kids in your classroom? Do you have higher, or lower, expectations for some than for others?**

We All Need Love

Say: **A basic need all children have is for the sense of significance that comes from experiencing unconditional love. Unconditional love is never based on performance. Unconditional love forgives. It keeps no record of wrongs. It always hopes for the best.**

There is one who loves our kids unconditionally. His name is Jesus. The children in our classrooms need us to show them and tell them:

Jesus forgives you and loves you—just the way you are!

With everyone still in small groups, ask:

● How can your expectations get in the way of showing unconditional love to all of your kids?

● What can you do to show more unconditional love to individual children in your class?

Division of Labor

Read aloud Psalm 86:5 and Psalm 103:10, 14.

Say: **In this world, we often are categorized by things we have little or no control over. Or we are branded by our past mistakes or sins. Fortunately, God does not categorize or brand us. Through Jesus, he forgives us and loves us just the way we are.**

He also loves us too much to let us stay that way! But we don't have to worry—he's a big God, and changing our hearts is his job.

With all of the accolades that Billy Graham has received over the years, you might think that this famous evangelist would have developed an oversized ego. But when his wife, Ruth, was asked if she ever needed to help her husband remain humble, she replied: "It's my job to keep Bill happy and God's job to make him good."

Ruth Graham is a wise woman. She knows that her role is simply to love Billy; it's God's job to change him.

Think of a child in your classroom who needs some special attention— maybe someone you'd like to change if you could. Now, silently fill in the blank in this sentence: "It's my job to love [child's name]. It's God's job to make him [or her] good."

Have the participants repeat the sentence aloud to the others in their small groups.

Say: **Now pray silently for the others in your group, asking God to help them show his unconditional love to the kids they teach.**

Healing Our Wounds

Have everyone return to the large group. Give each participant a bandage and a permanent marker.

Say: **Think about something in your own life that you feel branded by— maybe a personal shortcoming, a struggle, or a past event that has seemed to define you to yourself or others. Write that one thing on the pad side of your bandage (the part that usually goes against the wound). Then tape the bandage to your arm.**

As they do this, say: **The bandage is like God's love that shields you from** your own sin and shortcomings. No one ever needs to see what you wrote. God already knew. And the good news is: <u>Jesus forgives you and loves you—just the way you are!</u>

Think about using this bandage illustration with your students. Kids have tender hearts, and they know when they have done something wrong. They need to know that God forgives them, and they need to experience God's love and forgiveness through you!

Talking With God

Read aloud Colossians 3:13: **"Bear with each other and forgive whatever grievances you may have against one another. Forgive as the Lord forgave you."**

Say: **The more we recognize how much we are loved and forgiven by him, the more we can love and forgive others.** Think about someone who is difficult for you to love or maybe someone God has been telling you to forgive. This might be another adult or one of your students. I know that for some of you this will be very difficult. Take a moment and pray silently for God's help in loving and forgiving this person.

After a moment, close the prayer by saying: **Thank you, God, that <u>Jesus forgives us and loves us—just the way we are!</u> Amen.**

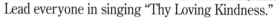

Lead everyone in singing "Thy Loving Kindness."

S E C T I O N
3

Devotions For Appreciation

♥ I Thank My God for You *DEC 2012*

Use this devotion to touch the hearts of your teachers, showing them how important their partnership in the gospel is to you, the kids, and God. Allow approximately ten minutes.

Words to Encourage People Who Love Kids

I thank my God for you!

─The Bible Basis─

"I thank my God every time I remember you. In all my prayers for all of you, I always pray with joy because of your partnership in the gospel from the first day until now, being confident of this, that he who began a good work in you will carry it on to completion until the day of Christ Jesus" (Philippians 1:3-6).

PREPARE FOR THIS SESSION

● Read Philippians 1:3-6, and spend time in prayer thanking God for the teachers and helpers he has sent to the children's ministry.

● Make bookmarks from strips of colored paper. Print: "[Teacher's name] is a partner in the gospel" on each one before laminating it or covering it with clear contact paper.

● Create a "Partnership Contract." Have someone draw up an official-looking "Partnership in the Gospel" contract full of legalese. Print one copy of the document on parchment for each teacher, put a huge gold seal on each, and have several of your church leaders sign each one.

● Ask your senior pastor and several elders (or other church leaders) to attend your meeting and be ready to pray for your staff members.

● Prepare to sing "Give Thanks" from *Group's Praise and Worship Songbook*.

● Arrange to hold this meeting in a beautifully decorated clubhouse at an apartment complex in your church's neighborhood or in a church member's home. Make it a classy evening by using fresh flowers and pretty balloon bouquets for decoration.

● Serve a mixture of small desserts, maybe fresh fruit and pastries. Ask a local bakery to make a special order of bite-sized treats.

A Biblical Blessing

Open the meeting by leading everyone to stand and sing "Give Thanks." Read aloud Philippians 1:3-6. Say: **I thank my God for you!**

From the First Day Until Eternity

Read or tell this true story:

Gladys was eighty-five when the new, wet-behind-the-ears, fresh-out-of-seminary children's pastor came to work at her church. Although he was only twenty-five years old, and she had taught Sunday school for sixty-five years at the same church, she was still his greatest encourager. Gladys never missed the monthly teacher training and planning meeting. She would always say, "If someone will come pick me up, I'll be there."

At the end of every training session, Gladys would tell the young pastor, "That was the best teacher training I've ever been to." She was a *very* gracious lady!

Gladys taught a class of fifth-graders. She was bound to the confines of a wheelchair by this time, but she never missed a Sunday with her kids.

Sometimes she fell asleep in class because her blood pressure medication never could be fine-tuned. But her kids loved her so much that they never left the room. They sat quietly until she awoke and pretended nothing had happened.

She finally had to have a younger lady assist her in the classroom, but she looked on this as a way of training a young woman to love kids and to teach them well.

The fifth-graders loved to gather around Gladys. As she arrived, they would argue over who got to push her wheelchair for her. She would tell them not to argue, but she knew that it was a sign of their love for her.

No one was absolutely sure, but the old-timers guessed that in her sixty-five years at the church, Gladys must have taught and touched the lives of more than two thousand children.

One Sunday, Gladys phoned the church office. She said she wasn't feeling well and wouldn't be able to make it to church to teach Sunday school that day. It was so uncharacteristic of her! The following Tuesday, Gladys went home to be with the Lord. Oh, how the angels—and Gladys too—must have rejoiced!

At her funeral, hundreds of people came to pay their respects. Pretty good for an elderly lady who lived alone for her entire life, never married, and outlived her whole family! But then, her family was made up of the hundreds and thousands of boys and girls she loved into the kingdom. And they loved her in return.

Gladys was a true partner in the gospel—from the first day until eternity. And the Lord continued to bless her as she taught. He continued to perform the good work he was doing in her life—just as he is doing in *yours*—until she went home to glory and the perfection that she told so many others was awaiting them!

Say: <u>I thank my God for you</u> because you are a Gladys in the making! I want each of you to remember that, along with Gladys, we are partners in the ministry of the gospel of Jesus Christ. I also want you to remember how much I appreciate you. So I made you each a "partnership Bible bookmark."

Hand the bookmarks to each teacher individually, saying: **Thank you,** [name], **and I appreciate you,** [name].

Partners in the Big Picture

Ask your senior pastor and other church leaders to come forward. Have the teachers stand. Say: **Your ministry is so important to our church. Our pastor and church leaders have joined us tonight to bless you and pray for you.** Allow time for the leaders to pray for each teacher individually or in small groups.

After the prayer, have the senior pastor present each teacher with a "Partnership Contract." He may also want to say a few words of appreciation to the whole group. Ask him to close by saying: <u>"I thank my God for you!"</u>

♥ *Flying High*

Use this devotion at a midyear meeting of your children's ministry staff to help them "fly high" as a committed team, understanding that their role is vital to the effectiveness of the ministry. Allow approximately fifteen minutes.

Words to Encourage People Who Love Kids

You have a vital role in children's ministry, and you're needed to complete the team!

> *"The body is a unit, though it is made up of many parts; and though all its parts are many, they form one body. So it is with Christ...But in fact God has arranged the parts in the body, every one of them, just as he wanted them to be. If they were all one part, where would the body be? As it is, there are many parts, but one body"* (1 Corinthians 12:12, 18-20).

PREPARE FOR THIS SESSION

● Read 1 Corinthians 12:12, 18-20, and think about how God has put together all the different "parts" of your children's ministry team.

● Make one copy of the photocopiable "Jesus Puzzle" (p. 59) for every five participants you expect to attend. Cut the pieces along the dotted lines, making sure to keep all the pieces of each puzzle together. (You may want to put each cut-up puzzle in its own plastic bag.)

● Set the Jesus puzzles on tables before the meeting, but remove one piece from each puzzle.

● On poster boards, overhead transparencies, or a flip chart, print the five "Truths About Teams" from the section "A Biblical Challenge From the World of Geese" in this devotion.

● Decorate your room with a nature or hunting theme. Use stuffed birds or decoys, plaid flannel table covers, and centerpieces of feathers and dried leaves.

● If the weather is cool, have a snack of hot soup and crackers (hearty stuff to take the chill off any outdoorsman or outdoorswoman). If the weather is warm, make a cool treat of mixed nuts and iced tea. If your budget can handle it, treat your staff to goose pâté!

Picture Perfect

As participants arrive, ask them to work together in groups of four or five to assemble one of the Jesus puzzles. Say: **I'll give you about three minutes to assemble your puzzle so that I can see the face of Jesus!**

Once people start complaining about the discovery of the missing pieces, say: **I removed one piece from each puzzle on purpose. Think about the experience you just had as you answer these questions.**

Ask the group at large for responses to the following questions:

● **What happens to the picture of Jesus when just one piece is missing?** (The puzzle is incomplete; you can't see the face of Jesus.)

● **How is your experience with this puzzle like or unlike our children's ministry when someone is missing?** (It's frustrating; the kids can't see the "face" of Jesus as well; it's incomplete.)

Say: **God calls each one of us to play a specific role in the body of Christ. When we all do our parts and serve in the capacity for which God** created us, the world sees a beautiful picture of Jesus. But without us in our appointed places, the body doesn't show the face of Christ—at least not as well. It can keep going, but it is not as effective.

You have a vital role in children's ministry, and you're needed to complete the team!

A Biblical Challenge from the World of Geese

Read aloud 1 Corinthians 12:12, 18-20.

Say: **Milton Olson is a naturalist whose study of geese has contributed much to our understanding of their behavior. Interestingly, geese have a lot to teach us about how to work together in the body of Christ and especially as partners in children's ministry in the local church.**

Step 1—Have each group of five stand and arrange themselves in a V-shaped formation, all facing toward the "point person." Say: **We're going to pretend that we are geese flying north in a V-shaped formation. So spread out your arms and start flapping your wings. Don't stop flying—we don't want anyone to fall out of the sky!**

Truth 1 About Geese. Say: **Have you ever wondered why geese fly in V-shaped formations when they migrate north for the summer and south for the winter? Scientists have learned that each bird benefits from the updraft of the bird in front of it. As each bird flaps its wings, it creates lift for the bird following it. When geese fly in this formation, they can fly over 70 percent farther than one bird could fly alone.**

Truth 1 About Teams. Display the corresponding poster or chart while you read: **"There are different kinds of gifts, but the same Spirit. There are different kinds of service, but the same Lord. There are different kinds of working, but the same God works all of them in all men. Now to each one the manifestation of the Spirit is given for the common good" (1 Corinthians 12:4-7).**

Say: **When the members of the body of Christ work together as we were designed to do by God, we all benefit, and we are more effective in our ministry of teaching and discipling children. Working together makes our jobs easier.**

Step 2—Have the last person on one side of the V pull out of formation and stand alone. Ask that person to continue flapping and also to start jumping up and down on both legs. Say: **You must continue flapping and jumping as long as you are out of formation. See what you get for being independent!**

Truth 2 About Geese. Say: **Geese learn quickly that if they separate themselves from the formation, they must work much harder to maintain their speed. The drag from flying through the air alone convinces the lone goose to return to the formation and the benefit of flying in another's uplift.**

Tell the loners they can return to their groups.

🦢 **Truth 2 About Teams.** Display the poster and read: **"All these are the work of one and the same Spirit, and he gives them to each one, just as he determines. The body is a unit, though it is made up of many parts; and though all its parts are many, they form one body. So it is with Christ"** (1 Corinthians 12:11-12).

Say: **When we work together in teams, supporting each other in our ministry to children, we all gain momentum and benefit from the ideas and encouragement of others. It is good to know we are not alone in ministry!**

Step 3—Have each point person rotate back into the tail of the V. Ask the other people to shift forward with one person becoming the new point.

🦢 **Truth 3 About Geese.** Say: **When the goose which is leading the V needs rest, it falls back, and another goose is ready and willing to take the leadership position. The former leader may then benefit from the restful updraft of another goose.**

🦢 **Truth 3 About Teams.** Display the poster and read: **"If the whole body were an eye, where would the sense of hearing be? If the whole body were an ear, where would the sense of smell be? But in fact God has arranged the parts in the body, every one of them, just as he wanted them to be"** (1 Corinthians 12:17-18).

Say: **God does not intend for us to be "lone rangers" in the ministry, doing everything ourselves. It is wise to share the hard work of being in charge with other members of the team.**

Step 4—Have all of the people behind the new leaders make a honking noise.

🦢 **Truth 4 About Geese.** Say: **When you hear geese honking as they fly, remember: That's their way of telling the leaders to keep going. You know, sometimes geese are better encouragers than Christians are!**

🦢 **Truth 4 About Teams.** Display the poster and read: **"Obey your leaders and submit to their authority. They keep watch over you as men who must give an account. Obey them so that their work will be a joy, not a burden, for that would be of no advantage to you"** (Hebrews 13:17).

Say: **Remember to pray for and encourage the people who lead you. God desires that we all do our part in making the job of leadership a joy.**

Step 5—Have the groups decide which member of each flock is the most tired. Say: **The one who is the most tired can sit down.** After a pause, tell everyone that they can stop flapping and sit down.

🦢 **Truth 5 About Geese.** Say: **Geese know how to support a weaker member of the flock. When a goose must drop out of the formation because it is sick or hurt, two other geese stay behind with it until it is either ready to fly—or dies.**

🦢 **Truth 5 About Teams.** Display the poster and read: **"If one part suffers, every part suffers with it; if one part is honored, every part rejoices** with it. Now you are the body of Christ, and each one of you is a part of it" (1 Corinthians 12:26-27).

Say: **Our ministry must include caring about each other when we are hurting or in need.**

Applying the Truths About Geese

Ask the groups of four or five to discuss together their answers to the following questions:

● **How did you feel being a part of this team of "geese"?**

● **How is this like or unlike the way our children's ministry team works together?**

● **Which of the five "Truths About Teams" means the most to you?**

● **Thinking about the "Truths About Teams," how can you help the teachers and helpers around you function more like a team, more like the way God wants the body of Christ to function?**

Say: <u>**You have a vital role in children's ministry, and you're needed to complete the team!**</u>

Talking With God

Say: **Think about the people you work with in ministry—your team.** Now think about your answer to the last question—how you're going to help your team function better. **Pray silently for your team members, and ask God to help you accomplish what you are committing to do.**

After several minutes of quiet prayer, close by saying: **Thank you, God, for each of these team members you have provided—because we need each one of them! Thank you for their willingness to fill such a vital role in our children's ministry. Amen.**

♥ A-Fishing We Will Go

Use this devotion at a teacher appreciation social to give your teachers a "big catch" of affirmation for helping "land" kids for the Lord! You could also use this to kick-off a training meeting on sharing the gospel message with children. Allow approximately ten to fifteen minutes.

Jesus Puzzle

Words to Encourage People Who Love Kids

Let's catch kids for Jesus!

The Bible Basis

" 'Come, follow me,' Jesus said, 'and I will make you fishers of men' "
(Matthew 4:19).

PREPARE FOR THIS SESSION

● Read Matthew 4:19, and think about the significance of Jesus' call to the children's ministry at your church.

● Gather your supplies: a blue bedsheet, a toy fishing rod, and a paper clip. Make a hook by bending the paper clip; then attach it to the end of the fishing line.

● Prepare a personalized affirmation card for each teacher using the photocopiable Love Note 4 (p. 88). You might attach a small gift such as a small "fish" lapel pin from your local Christian bookstore.

Write a personalized message telling each worker about something you've observed them doing that helps catch kids for Jesus. Or write something like, "When it comes to catching kids for Jesus, you make good bait!" or "Thanks for having the patience of an angler when you're working with our kids!"

Use a hole punch to put one hole at the top of each card. Place the cards in a bag under a table at the front of the room.

● Prepare to sing or play a recording of the children's song "I Will Make You Fishers of Men." Also, you could play two songs by Mary Rice Hopkins: "Gonna Go Fishin' " and "The Fish Are Gonna Bite" from the CD or cassette *In My Garden: Sowing Seeds of Love.*

● Gather some fishing equipment for decorating your room. Use items such as fishing rods and reels, tackle boxes, waders, lures, and mounted fish. Hang the items on the wall, or place them around the room. Consider leading the devotion while wearing waders and a fishing hat.

● During your meeting, allow everyone to snack from bowls of fish-shaped crackers. Later, for a special treat, serve "Fish Tanks" made of blue gelatin in clear plastic cups with gummy fish "swimming" around inside.

The Littlest Fisherman

As teachers are arriving, sing or play the children's song "I Will Make You Fishers of Men."

Read or tell this true story:

Eric, a young Christian father, took his two small daughters fishing in a Dallas reservoir. After several hours without even a bite, the father decided he needed to redeem the time by calling the girls' attention to the spiritual parallel of "fishing for men."

The father asked Amanda, his six-year-old, if she remembered the story in the Bible where Jesus said that if we followed him, he would make us fishers of men.

"Yes, Daddy, I remember," she said.

The father asked the girl what she thought the story meant, and Amanda correctly responded that Jesus would use us like "bait" to attract non-Christians to God and help them believe.

A long silence followed while Eric reflected on the brilliance of his young daughter.

Then Amanda said, "Daddy, can we go to the other side of the pond? I remember another story in the Bible where Jesus said to cast your line on the other side—and it ended up working a lot better than this!"

Say: There are lots of little Amandas out there. Some of them would amaze us with what they already understand about God. Others still need to hear the good news. Let's catch kids for Jesus!

A Biblical Challenge

Have your workers form groups of three or four. Read aloud Matthew 4:19.

Say: Jesus was talking to two brothers, Peter and Andrew, who were fishermen by trade. It's interesting to note that the phrase "Come, follow me" is a command, not a request.

Ask the following questions and have the groups discuss their answers:

● How would you have felt if Jesus had asked *you* to leave your occupation and family business to follow him?

● What would you have done?

Say: The next verse tells us how Peter and Andrew responded.

Read Matthew 4:20: "At once they left their nets and followed him."

Ask everyone to reflect silently on their answers to these questions:

● Is there anything that you've had to give up to teach children about Jesus?

● Is there anything that you're still holding on to—an attitude, a commitment, a sinful habit—that keeps you from following Jesus more closely and ministering more effectively?

● Do you trust that Jesus will fulfill his promise to make you "fishers of men"—that is, to "catch kids for Jesus?"

The Fish Will Bite

Ask two of your lead teachers to come forward. Have them stretch out the blue sheet in front of the table at the front of the room and hold the ends at shoulder height so the sheet is tight and hangs to the floor.

Go behind the sheet, draw one of your personalized affirmation cards from the bag under the table, and call out the name of the person on the card. Have that person take up the toy fishing rod and hang the line over the top of the sheet. Attach the person's affirmation card. Continue to call new anglers until everyone has caught a card. Ask two people who've already had a turn to hold the sheet while your two leaders get a turn to fish.

LEADER TIP:

If you have a large group, use several fishing rods and call two or three anglers at a time.

While this activity is going on, play one or both Mary Rice Hopkins songs—"Gonna Go Fishin'" and "The Fish Are Gonna Bite"—as background music.

Talking With God

Have everyone turn to a partner and share the names of two or three children in their classrooms with whom they would like to share the gospel. Have the partners pray for each other and the children. (Offer to pray with anyone who does not have a partner, or have the person join one of the twosomes.)

 Close the time of prayer by saying: **Thank you, God, for these willing workers who have given their lives to <u>catch kids for Jesus!</u> Amen.**

♥ *Trend-Setting Teens*

Use this devotion at a gathering of young helpers (late elementary through high school age) to show your sincere appreciation for their willingness to serve—and to challenge them to direct their spiritual vitality into new levels of trend-setting ministry. Allow approximately fifteen to twenty minutes.

Words to Encourage People Who Love Kids

Thanks for being trendsetters!

PREPARE FOR THIS SESSION

● Read 1 Timothy 4:11-12, and pray that God will give your teenage helpers the grace to be examples to younger children in their classrooms—and to the whole church.

● Gather your supplies: a penny; a pocket calculator; and a large, one-month calendar.

● Photocopy and cut apart the Bible Story Strips (p. 66). Fold the strips, and put them in a hat or a can.

● Make a list of your teen helpers' names and a specific quality or act of service that you appreciate about each of them.

● Decorate your room with posters of popular Christian recording artists (ask the youth ministry at your church to help you out). Be sure to have a CD player, and ask the teens to bring some of their favorite Christian CDs.

● There's only one choice for this meeting's snack—pizza. We suggest pepperoni, with Dr Pepper to drink. While you're eating, listen to the kids' CDs or watch Christian music videos.

A Penny That's Worth a Million

Hold up one penny. Ask: **If you were given a choice between receiving a penny now and having it doubled every day for thirty days, or waiting thirty days and being given $1 million, which would you choose?**

Have the teens raise their hands to indicate their choice. Allow some rivalry and tension to develop between those who choose the first option and those who choose the second. Most of your teens will probably choose the $1 million.

Say: **Although taking the $1 million seems like a good choice, those of you who chose the penny would have made the better long-term investment. Now, you may not think so at first. But it's true.**

Give one of your teens a calculator and have that person follow along with your calculations to verify what you are saying. Display the large calendar, and begin by writing "$1 million or...?" on the last day of the month. Then mark your calculations for the penny-doubling on each day until you reach the end of the month. (For example, one cent doubled equals two cents on the first day; two cents doubled equals four cents on the second day; four cents doubled equals eight cents on the third day; and so on.)

Say: **After ten days, the penny would have grown to a mere $5.12. Even** after twenty days, you might think you had made a mistake by not taking the $1 million since your total would be just $5,242.88. But after thirty days, you would be the wiser investor with $5,368,709.12.

Ask the teens to turn to a partner and discuss their answers to these questions (a teen who does not have a partner can join a twosome):

● How did you feel about being asked to make such a choice (especially if you were in the minority)?

● How did you feel after finding out how far a penny can go?

● How is this like or unlike having to make mature decisions about what you will do with your life? (It was hard; there were big consequences; I didn't want to just go along with the crowd; it was hard to think about being patient for the big payoff.)

Ask: How will you invest your life? Are you willing to be patient and diligent with the little things in order to gain the long-term rewards of the Christian life? Are you willing to stand firm against the crowd to be an example of how to live?

Say: Some of you were pretty fearless in choosing the unpopular "investment strategy." At times in your Christian life, you will be faced with some pretty unpopular choices. You are already making wise, mature choices by committing some of your time and energy to work with the children at church.

You are true trendsetters! A trendsetter is someone who establishes a course that others follow. You are setting a standard for living the Christian life—not only for other teens and kids, but for the adults in this church as well. Thank you for being trendsetters!

A Biblical Challenge

Read aloud 1 Timothy 4:11-12. Ask the teens to turn to their partners again and discuss their answers to these questions:

● Why do you think Paul wrote these verses to Timothy?

● How can you set a Christian trend for other people to follow?

● Is it harder to model the Christian life for older people, people your own age, or younger people? Why?

● Why does your age sometimes hold you back from leading, teaching, or modeling the Christian life?

● Who is someone for whom *you* can serve as a trendsetter for living the Christian life?

Trend-Setting Mimes

Say: The Bible gives us many examples of kids and teenagers who were real trendsetters for their times. We're going to act out some of their stories.

If you have a smaller group, have each person draw one Bible Story Strip from the hat or can. If you have a larger group, ask several teens to share a strip and work together.

Say: **I'll give you three minutes to read the Scripture passage and come up with ideas for acting it out—without using any words! The rest of us will try to guess what the story is.**

After each teen or group has had a turn and each story has been correctly identified, ask: **How do you think the young star of the story was a trendsetter?**

Make sure these points are brought out:

● Mary was just a young teenager when she discovered she was an unwed mother carrying a miracle baby. She was a trendsetter for having faith in God.

● The little boy with the loaves and fish was just a poor child. He was a trendsetter for sharing what little he had with others and with God, who was then able to use his generosity to bless thousands.

● Joseph had a rough start in life, but he used his gifts and his obedience to God to grow up in the Lord and be a national leader who would save God's people from starvation.

● Daniel was a sharp young man whom many envied and despised for his giftedness. (Some of your most-promising teens may experience this in school or even at church.) Even so, he was a trendsetter in standing firm for his convictions, and he ended up convincing even the king to believe in his God!

● By trusting God and refusing to bow down to the king, Shadrach, Meshach, and Abednego, who were young men, showed Nebuchadnezzar and all his people the great power of the living God. They started a new trend in their country of worshipping the true God—even gaining legal protection for those who did!

● David didn't just protect his people by killing the giant; he also set an amazing example for the many adults who watched him live victoriously because of his trust in God.

Say: **This game has been fun. I hope some of these Bible trendsetters have inspired you and set examples for you to follow, because you are real leaders in our church. I'm very proud of the ways that you set an example for ministry in our church. Thanks for being trendsetters!**

Talking With God

Close the meeting in a prayer of thanksgiving for the spiritual maturity you see developing in your trend-setting teen helpers. Mention each teen by name, thanking God for a specific quality or act of service that you appreciate.

BIBLE STORY STRIPS

- Mary discovering that she was pregnant with Jesus **(Luke 1:26-38)**.

- The little boy offering Jesus his small lunch of fish and barley loaves to feed a crowd **(John 6:1-13)**.

- Joseph, who was hated by his brothers, being thrown into a pit and sold into slavery **(Genesis 37:3-36)**.

- Daniel ending up in the lions' den after refusing to stop praying to God **(Daniel 6:6-28)**.

- Shadrach, Meshach, and Abednego refusing to bow down before the king and ending up in the fiery furnace **(Daniel 3:1-30)**.

- Young David killing Goliath with a slingshot after all the adults proved too afraid to fight the giant **(1 Samuel 17:20-52)**.

4

DeVotions For SPeCiaL EVents

♥ We Have Finished the Race

Use this devotion to honor and praise your teachers and helpers as you celebrate the conclusion of a major event such as vacation Bible school, summer camp, or the Sunday school year. Allow approximately ten minutes.

Words to Encourage People Who Love Kids

We kept on going, and we finished the race!

The Bible Basis

"I have fought the good fight, I have finished the race, I have kept the faith. Now there is in store for me the crown of righteousness, which the Lord, the righteous Judge, will award to me on that day—and not only to me, but also to all who have longed for his appearing" (2 Timothy 4:7-8).

PREPARE FOR THIS SESSION

● Read 2 Timothy 4:7-8, and thank God for all of the workers who "finished the race" with you. You couldn't have done it without them!

● Gather your supplies: a ribbon long enough to string across the meeting room doorway; a recording of the theme song from the Olympic Games or the movie *Chariots of Fire;* a flashlight; a piece of red, yellow, or orange cellophane; and (optional) taped applause.

● Make a "torch" by taping the colored cellophane to the lighted end of the flashlight and turning the light on.

● Decorate your room with posters of athletes, especially Olympic medal winners and other runners crossing finish lines, if possible. Make torches for your tables by putting small flashlights inside paper towel tubes and covering the ends with red, yellow or orange cellophane.

LEADER TIP:

Why not rent the video *Chariots of Fire* and play a clip of the famous race scene as a part of your devotion? Or have a party and show the whole movie, pausing for a half time devotion and snack break.

● For a snack, serve a sports drink and high-energy bars or granola. (You know—good-for-you kinds of stuff that athletes like us are supposed to eat!)

The Finish Line

After most or all of your teachers and helpers have arrived, have them exit the room and prepare to re-enter one at a time.

Have two of your leaders hold the ribbon tightly across the doorway. With the theme music playing in the background, have the workers re-enter as you announce their name and ministry position or contribution. Allow them to "break through" the finish line by having the leaders drop one end of the ribbon each time. Have everyone cheer and applaud for one another. (You might even add taped applause.)

Once everyone has been seated again, say: **We kept on going, and we finished the race!** Lead everyone in one more round of applause for the group effort and for God's accomplishment.

God Made Him Fast

Tell or read the true story of Eric Liddell, as portrayed in the Oscar-winning movie, *Chariots of Fire:*

Eric Liddell was fast, and he used his speed to bring attention to God. Against the wishes of his sister, who wanted him to give up running to focus on the more "important" work of the family's mission to China, Eric trained hard and eventually was granted a place on the Olympic track team from Great Britain. He was to represent his country and his God in Paris at the Eighth Olympiad Games in 1924.

As a way of explaining his desire to run, he told his sister, "I believe that God made me for a purpose...for China. He also made me fast. And when I run, I feel his pleasure. To give it up would be to hold him in contempt. You were right. It's not just fun. To win is to honor him."

Eric's father supported his running. He told Eric: "You can praise the Lord by peeling a potato if you peel it to perfection. Run in his [God's] name and let the world stand back in wonder."

Often, after winning a competition, Eric would gather contestants and crowd members together to share the gospel. He compared running in a race to his own faith. There's no formula for winning, he explained, because everyone has to run the race in his own way. But the rules are clear, and the end is worth the work.

After his appointment to the British Olympic team, Eric was puzzled to discover that the heat for his Olympic event, the one hundred-meter race, would be held on a Sunday—the one day he could not compete because

of his strong convictions about honoring the Sabbath. Although he was pressured by British officials and royalty to run anyway, he would not compromise his beliefs. He stepped out of the competition.

But thanks to Andrew Lindsay, who had taken a silver medal in another race, Eric's Olympic dream was not over. Lindsay gave up his spot in the four hundred-meter race (which was being run on another day) to give Eric a chance to compete.

Although Eric was known as a sprinter, he actually was well-suited to longer distances, too. In this new event, Eric ran very fast—and he earned the Olympic gold medal.

Because of Eric's stand for the Lord, his testimony went on to be told to thousands. The movie telling his story, *Chariots of Fire,* ended up winning the Academy Award for Best Picture.

After the Olympics, Eric returned to his family's work sharing the gospel in China. He died in a prison camp in occupied China just before the end of World War II. But his story lives on.

Say: **Just like Eric Liddell <u>we kept on going, and we finished the race!</u>**

A Biblical Challenge

Read aloud 2 Timothy 4:7-8. Ask participants to get into groups of three or four and discuss the following questions:

● **How does it make you feel to know that we have finished a great project for God?**

● **How did you "keep the faith" and finish this project?**

● **How does it make you feel to hear Paul's words about God granting you a crown of righteousness?**

● **How was the experience of this** [vacation Bible school, church camp, Sunday school semester] **like or unlike the Christian life that Paul describes as a race or a fight?** (It was different because we had a clear ending point in sight; it was similar because it pleased God; in both cases we have to keep going and keep our faith that what we're doing is for God's purpose.)

Talking With God

Pick up the torch you made, and turn it on. Say: **We're going to take turns thanking God for one thing he has accomplished during this "marathon" we have just completed. I'll go first. Thank you, God, for** [name an accomplishment].

Then hand the torch to one of the workers nearest you. Say: [Name], **please**

stand and thank God for one thing you saw him accomplish during this ministry project.

Have the torch pass from person to person, giving everyone a turn to share a "thank you." Lead the group in applause after each thanksgiving.

♥ Little Children, Lambs of God

Use this devotional in a congregational meeting as a teacher dedication or commissioning service, or use it in a kickoff meeting for new volunteers. Touch the hearts of your staff and congregation as you ask them to commit to caring for God's little lambs. Allow approximately ten minutes.

Words to Encourage People Who Love Kids

Jesus says, "Feed my sheep!"

The Bible Basis

"Be shepherds of God's flock that is under your care, serving as overseers—not because you must, but because you are willing, as God wants you to be...And when the Chief Shepherd appears, you will receive the crown of glory that will never fade away" (1 Peter 5:2a, 4).

PREPARE FOR THIS SESSION

● Read 1 Peter 5:2a, 4, and think about its implications for your own ministry.

● Take a roll of slides with tight, close-up pictures of a baby's face. Dress the baby in a lamb's costume, or have the baby's face showing through a cardboard cutout of a lamb that you create.

As an alternative, find pictures of real lambs. Glue face shots of your church's babies over the heads of the lambs in the pictures; then photograph these creations for your slide show.

● Arrange for a time in a Sunday service when all of the children of the church can parade into the sanctuary with their teachers.

● Have each child prepare a hand-held "lamb mask" in advance. For each mask, draw a lamb's face on a

LEADER TIP:

If you can find a live lamb, ask its owner to bring it in on the day of the commissioning. Have a pastor or lead teacher dress up as a shepherd, stand outside the church entrance next to the lamb, and welcome everyone to the service!

paper plate. Glue cotton balls and construction paper ears to the plate, and attach a craft stick holder.

● Prepare to have the congregation sing songs from your hymnal, such as "Savior Like a Shepherd Lead Us," that remind us of Jesus, the Good Shepherd.

● If the teacher dedication is part of a worship service, plan to host a reception for your volunteers afterward. Decorate a room with stuffed toy sheep and shepherd's crooks. Have the children make cotton-ball sheep pictures to hang on the walls.

● For a snack, serve ice cream "lambs." Roll a vanilla ice cream ball in shredded coconut, and place it in a plastic bowl. Make two lamb's ears out of two halves of a vanilla wafer cookie. Use a pink jelly bean for the nose and two black jelly beans for the eyes.

Sheep Like Us

As you begin the commissioning, project your "lamb" baby pictures onto a large screen at the front of the room. Read aloud 1 Peter 5:2a, 4.

Say to the congregation (or to your gathering of volunteers): **Have you ever wondered why God refers to us as sheep? Well, there are some interesting parallels between domesticated sheep and human beings.**

For one, sheep are very *valuable.* **In fact, they're among the most valuable of all domesticated animals around the world. They provide humans with meat, milk, cheese, and wool.**

They are also very *vulnerable.* **Domesticated sheep must rely upon their masters to keep them from being harmed by predators and other dangers. They are easily frightened, often terrified en masse by a piece of paper blowing in the wind or a loud crack of thunder. They can be killed easily when frightened, since they are so quick to follow one another in a panic— even when the leader is running into the danger instead of away from it.**

In the same way, the little children who we shepherd at this church— through the teachers and workers we're honoring today—are precious little lambs, and they are vulnerable to attack and to dangers from all sides. Because they are so precious to God, we are commanded by him to take good care of them. Jesus says, "Feed my sheep!"

The Parade of the Flock

Have the congregation sing "Gentle Shepherd" or "Savior Like a Shepherd Lead Us." During the song, have all of the children of the church parade into the sanctuary with their teachers and helpers. Have the kids hold their lamb masks a few inches in front of their faces.

Challenging the Shepherds

Have the children and teachers stand together at the front of the room. Say: **Teachers, I am going to ask you a series of questions. If you agree with them, please respond with, "I will."**

● **Will you be willing shepherds of God's flock that is under your care as God wants you to be?** (I will.)

● **Will you cherish the little lambs under your care, always recognizing their great value to the Good Shepherd?** (I will.)

● **Will you protect the sheep that God has placed under your care, guiding them to truth and away from danger?** (I will.)

Say: **Jesus says, "Feed my sheep!"**

Optional: Have the senior pastor "present" a live lamb to the children's ministry director, saying, "This lamb is a reminder to you as the leader of our children's ministry to care for the flock. Jesus says, 'Feed my sheep!'"

Talking With the Chief Shepherd

Say: **Thank you, God, for these wonderful, willing children's workers. Please guide each one in his or her ministry. Remember them and your promise that "when the Chief Shepherd appears, [we] will receive the crown of glory that will never fade away." Amen.**

♥ Stand Firm

Use this devotion at the kickoff of a new season of ministry to encourage "old" and "new" teachers alike to make a solid commitment to a life of ministry before God. Allow approximately twenty minutes.

Words to Encourage People Who Love Kids

Your labor for God is never in vain!

The Bible Basis

"Therefore, my dear brothers, stand firm. Let nothing move you. Always give yourselves fully to the work of the Lord, because you know that your labor in the Lord is not in vain" (1 Corinthians 15:58).

PREPARE FOR THIS SESSION

● Read 1 Corinthians 15:58, and be encouraged to stand firm in your own ministry.

● Gather your supplies: one deck of playing cards for every three or four people, and a portable hair dryer.

● Prepare to sing the old Sunday school favorite "The Wise Man Built His House Upon the Rock."

● Prepare a large batch of "pud" by mixing water and baking soda until it is the texture of peanut butter. Make enough to give each participant two or three tablespoonfuls.

● Decorate your room by placing small tubs of sand on your tables. Build simple card houses in the sand. (To provide support, you can tape the cards together, or tape them to the outside of a small box.)

● For a snack, serve "reinforced" flavored gelatin squares. Make a batch of flavored gelatin using less water than the recipe calls for (use 1½ cups of boiling water for two three-ounce packages of gelatin dessert). After that batch is firm, add a layer of a different flavor in the same pan. Let it become firm. Make several layers.

Cut the finished dessert into cubes; then thread the cubes onto skewers. Put two or three cubes on each skewer with marshmallows or fruit chunks in between. (The skewer is like the reinforcement bar giving added strength to block buildings—or like the Spirit of God helping us "stand firm" even when we're a little "jiggly" in our own strength!)

A Biblical Challenge

Say: **Do you ever become discouraged in ministry? Do you ever become frustrated with your attempt to live the Christian life? We all do. But we need to remember that because we have great hope in the resurrection and a hope for the future, you and I have been given a real incentive for serving God now. Your labor for God is never in vain!**

Read aloud 1 Corinthians 15:58.

Have participants form groups of three or four, and give each group a deck of playing cards.

Say: **I want each group to work together to build the tallest or the most elaborate house of cards that you can. I'll give you five minutes.**

When time is up, pull out a portable hair dryer (you may need to plug it into a long extension cord). Go around the room and blow down each group's structure, ignoring the groans and protests.

Ask everyone to share their answers to these questions with their group:

● **How did it make you feel to work so hard on your house of cards only to have it senselessly blown down?**

● How is this like or unlike our own Christian walks? our work in children's ministry? (Sometimes all of our efforts seem to be in vain; results seem short-lived; we want to quit.)

Don't Be Moved

Ask everyone to stand. Say: **In your groups, choose one person to "stand firm." That person will plant his or her feet and not move, no matter what! Now, the rest of the group is going to try to get that person to move. You can do anything you can think of to try to move that person except touching him or her.**

After a minute or two, have the people in each group switch places. Give each participant an opportunity to stand firm. Then have everyone share their answers to the following questions with their groups:

● **How did you feel about trying to stand firm while your opponents tried to make you move?**

● **How is this like or unlike the ways we are challenged to give up or compromise in our Christian walk or ministry?**

● **What are some challenges that tempt us to not stand firm in our ministry to children?** (Busyness; frustration; too few volunteers; lack of appreciation.)

● **How can you stand firm?** (Work with a team; keep focused on God; pray.)

Say: **Don't give in! Stand firm. <u>Your labor for God is never in vain!</u>**

Firm or Flimsy?

Lead your group in singing "The Wise Man Built His House Upon the Rock." Give each participant one or two tablespoons of pud.

Say: **Roll your pud into a ball.** Wait for everyone to do this. **Now set your nice, firm ball down on the table.** (Pud holds its shape as long as pressure is being applied. Once it is set down, the ball will become a puddle.) Have participants repeat the process.

Ask for various people to share their answers to these questions:

● **What kept your pud in the shape you wanted?** (Pressure; you had to keep rolling it in a ball.)

● **What happened when you stopped rolling your pud?** (Its shape dissolved; the work we had done was in vain.)

● **How is setting the ball of pud down like or unlike giving up or not standing firm in the ministry or in life?** (A lot of the disciplined work we do in ministry or in our Christian life gets "undone" if we aren't diligent in keeping it up.)

● **What does this mean for your future in ministry at our church? for your future in your own spiritual life?**

Talking With God

Have participants spend time quietly thinking about their commitments to God and to the work of his ministry. Say: **Think back to those things you shared earlier that may be trying to push into your life—and to push ministry out. Share those things with God and ask for help in prioritizing them, handling them, or resisting them. Ask God to help you stand firm.**

Close the prayer by saying: **Thank you, God, for each of these wonderful people who are so vital to the children's ministry at our church. Help them to stand firm and to understand that <u>their labor for you is never in vain.</u> Amen.**

5

BONUS IDEAS TO ENCOURAGE PEOPLE WHO LOVE KIDS

Bonus Idea 1

Close-Up Appreciation

At the closing of any major children's program such as camps, club programs, or vacation Bible school, show a musical video presentation to your kids, volunteers, and parents. This can serve as a great recap of the week for the kids, an appreciation message to your teachers and helpers, and a positive recruiting plug for the parents.

Using a video camera, take occasional pictures during the program. Be sure to include as many close-ups of the faces of your kids and volunteers as possible. Include clips of kids hugging or thanking teachers. No narration is necessary—just play some upbeat music in the background when you show the video.

Close the presentation with a close-up of a group of kids holding a handmade poster. It should say something like, "Thank you for teaching us at [name of event or program]."

Bonus Idea 2

Caught in the Act!

Set a goal for yourself to affirm at least five of your children's workers each week.

Carry a miniature tape recorder in your pocket as you walk around during Sunday school or any other children's program. Watch for teachers or helpers doing good things, and record their names and what they did on your recorder. (Wait until you are out of view to do this!)

On Sunday afternoon or Monday morning, listen to your tape to remind yourself of the specific things you want to affirm. Write and mail thank you notes or use one of the Love Notes in Section 6 of this book. Be sure to mention the action you observed. Praise is more effective when it is specific!

Bonus Idea 3

For the Love of Children Month

Have a monthlong celebration at your church honoring children, families, and especially children's workers. Call it "For the Love of Children Month."

Focus the whole church on kids. Put a banner in the front of your sanctuary that reads, "For the Love of Children…" and include drawings or photographs of happy kids smiling and playing.

Run special articles in your church newsletter or bulletin about the children's ministry. Ask a different teacher or student to give a testimony in church each week. (Be sure to pick people who can express their excitement about ministry to kids.) Set up a table in the foyer with parenting helps, ideas, and resources for your congregation to browse through. Close the month with your annual teacher appreciation event.

Bonus Idea 4

High-Calorie Appreciation

Have an "open-house dessert" for your teachers.

Do away with the old "appreciation dinner" idea. Some people are very uncomfortable at formal banquets where they get stuck at a table all night with people they hardly know. Besides, dinners are expensive and lots of work!

Instead, have an informal, drop-in style dessert. Find a nice clubhouse at a local apartment or condo complex (or a nice, large home in your congregation). Set up a pastry bar or ice cream buffet. Let people eat and socialize at will.

With an advance order, most bakeries will make special snack-sized pastries that will save you money and will be easier for people to eat. Or arrange for a group of kids from the ministry to get together and make a special "thank you" dessert. Be sure to have optional fruit dishes for those who are trying to avoid sweets.

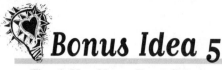

Bonus Idea 5

Thank You Notes From Parents and Kids

Have parents write thank you notes (or help their kids write them) to their children's teachers.

Send out a mailing to all the parents in your church, making sure to pull out the ones addressed to members of your children's ministry staff—after all, many of them are parents too! Send pre-printed stationery with clip art of kids and one of these slogans:

- "For the love of _____" leaving the blank to write the teacher's name.
- "_____...A teacher to remember."

Include in your mailing a list of all the people who help in each child's room so that none will be forgotten. Provide several sheets of stationery if you have multiple workers in each room or kids who attend more than one service.

Ask for the notes to be returned to you or the church office. Then group all of the notes for each teacher together, making sure that no one is overlooked. Present each teacher with this "bundle of affirmation" at an appreciation event or on a special Sunday.

Bonus Idea 6

Long-Stem Appreciation

One Sunday, surprise each teacher with an inexpensive carnation as he or she arrives. Yes, guys like getting flowers, too. They just won't admit it! (Besides, he can always give the flower to his wife and be a hero!)

Bonus Idea 7

Bravo Awards

Pop in on your teachers during their classroom times and give them individual "Bravo Awards." These could be any small food or convenience item that provides a surprise encouragement through a play on words. Attach a card to the item and write your praise. For example:

- For a teen helper, buy a packet of Kool-Aid drink mix and write, "Thanks for being a 'cool aide!' "

● For an administrative type, buy a box of Cracker Jack candied popcorn and write, "You're a 'crackerjack' at keeping us all organized!"

● Use one of the photocopiable Love Notes found in Section 6.

Pop into the classroom with an "appreciation committee" of two or three people and yell, "Bravo!" After you have everyone's attention, present your "Bravo Award" and tell why the worker is so special to you.

LEADER TIP:
Shop after the major "candy" holidays (Halloween, Christmas, Easter and Valentine's Day) for bags of miniature candy bars on sale.

Bonus Idea 8

The Teacher's Survival Kit

Fill a zippered plastic bag with one each of the following items: a rubber band, a tissue, a button, a toothpick, a bandage, a Hershey's Kisses chocolate candy, a gold thread, an eraser, a Life Savers candy, and a mint. Add a copy of the "Teacher's Survival Kit" (p.80).

Bonus Idea 9

Two Hugs for You!

Gather a plastic spoon, two Hershey's Hugs chocolate candies, colored cellophane, and a ribbon. Put the Hugs in the bowl of the spoon, cover the candy and spoon with the cellophane, and tie it with ribbon. Attach a note saying, "These hugs are for you. One's from Jesus. The other's from me." Give it to a teacher or helper who needs some extra encouragement.

Bonus Idea 10

A Thank You Plant for the Whole Family

Invite children's workers and their families to a potluck dinner or dessert party.

THE TEACHER'S SURVIVAL KIT

This kit is for you! Use it in your life and ministry.

➤ The rubber band is to thank you for all those times you give loving hugs to the kids—and to remind you that I'm hugging you back each time you love a child.

➤ The tissue is to help you dry one more child's tears—or maybe your own so you can see the tears of others more clearly. Remember that I weep along with you.

➤ The button is to remind you to "button your lip" when you would be justified in saying something to an unruly child or an angry parent but know it would be wiser to remain silent.

➤ The toothpick is to help you "pick out" the excellent qualities of your children and yourself. Remember that I'm not done with either of you yet!

➤ The bandage is to help you heal the hurts of your students—and your own. Remember that I was wounded for you.

➤ The Hershey's Kisses candy is because I know you like chocolate, and I like seeing you enjoy life!

➤ The gold thread is to help us tie our hearts together because my friendship with you is golden!

➤ The eraser is to remind you that everyone makes mistakes sometimes—and that's OK. Be ready to forgive your kids and yourself, just as I have forgiven you.

➤ The Life Savers candy means you are a "lifesaver" in this ministry, and because I want you to think of me as your lifesaver whenever you need to cry out for help. Remember that I'm always listening.

➤ The mint is to remind you that you are worth a "mint" to me!

Love, Jesus

Before the party, purchase small plants from a local nursery or grocery store for each family and use the plants to decorate the room. Wrap each pot with bright foil and a big bow. Place a "flag" with a family's name on it in each pot. Include a message such as "Thanks for helping grow our kids" or "You're planting seeds for eternity."

At the end of the evening, have the families find their plants and take them home. Be sure to tell spouses and kids how much you appreciate the gift *they* give by letting Mom or Dad work in the children's ministry at church!

 Bonus Idea 11

You're 'Key' to The Ministry!

This idea can take a whole week if you want to do it all!

● Mail each teacher a copy of Love Note 12 (p. 92), or during a Sunday school session or a teacher's meeting, hand a note to each teacher. Tape an old key to the card, with a ribbon or safety pin threaded through the keyhole. Ask the teachers to wear the key to church the next week and be ready to tell people what the key represents—that the children's ministry is the "key" ministry at the church and the teachers are "key" to the ministry.

● Use your church newsletter or another mailing to ask parents to bring old keys to church the next Sunday morning and give the keys to their children's teachers as tokens of appreciation.

Another option is to ask the congregation to gather keys and bring them to a worship service for a special dedication. Have your senior pastor ask all of the children's ministry teachers and helpers to come forward at some point during the service. Have the rest of the congregation come down and present keys to the teachers to say "thanks."

> **LEADER TIP:**
> Stand in the hallway near your children's classrooms with a bag of keys to hand out to parents who forget.

One more option is to take a special "offering," passing the offering plates and collecting keys. Have your ushers unload the offering trays or bags onto the front platform or a small table. Have the senior pastor ask all of the children's workers to stand in their places while the children's ministry director comes forward. The pastor can then present the keys to the director, standing in proxy for the whole team.

The goal is to inundate the teachers with keys to help them recognize the abundance of appreciation the church has for their important work.

Bonus Idea 12

Mother's Day Celebration

Take the outside wrapper off of a Hershey's chocolate bar, leaving the foil cover on the chocolate. Make up your own wrapper, decorating it with a frilly red heart and these words: "Happy Mother's Day! Thank you for being a 'mom' every week to some very special kids at our church. Your ministry is changing lives!"

Present a re-wrapped chocolate bar to every female staff member working on Mother's Day. Be sure to include substitutes, teenagers, singles, and married women without kids. They're all "mothering" kids at church!

Bonus Idea 13

Father's Day Celebration

Buy enough Big Hunk candy bars to give one to every male worker in your program. Attach a certificate to each bar that reads: "Thanks for giving up some of your week to be a positive male role model for kids who need to know it's cool to be a man and love Jesus!"

Bonus Idea 14

LEADER TIP:

This will quickly become your best place to find staff members when you want to distribute newsletters or information.

Sunday Morning Doughnuts and Coffee

No doubt it's hard for some of your teachers and helpers to get out of the house on time on Sunday mornings. Why not help them by providing a welcome snack just for children's ministry workers? Set up a coffee pot, an iced tea pitcher, and a tray of doughnuts in your children's ministry office or resource room. (You might ask parents who aren't working in the ministry to provide an occasional tray of goodies.) Be ready for the first teacher to arrive!

Bonus Idea 15

Secret Pals

Put every worker's name on a slip of paper in a basket. Then pass the basket at a staff meeting, and have everyone draw the name of a "secret pal." Or enlist secret pals by distributing the names of your volunteers to parents and others who are not working in your ministry.

Suggest that secret pals surprise their teachers or helpers with encouraging notes and small goodies. Set up some guidelines for how long the program will last (we suggest three to six months) and how much can be spent on gifts (usually no more than five dollars per month). It really *is* the thought that counts!

At the end of the program, throw a "Pal Party," and let everyone find out who their secret pals have been.

Bonus Idea 16

Prayer Partners

Make a "Prayer Partners" chart at the beginning of a Sunday school term, before vacation Bible school starts, or before a special camp or retreat. Include all the names of your volunteers on the chart, with two or three blanks by each name. Then ask parents and the congregation at large to pick one or more workers for whom they will pray, and have them write their names on lines next to the workers' names. When your staff members learn that specific people are praying for them, they will be encouraged!

Bonus Idea 17

I'm Praying for You

Pray for five of your teachers each week; then drop them a note telling them you did. If possible, have other people such as the pastor or your ministry leaders pray with you. Using Love Note 1 (p. 87), write a simple message such as, "We prayed for you and your ministry this week. Thanks for all you do!" Have everyone who prayed sign the card; then drop it in the mail.

Bonus Idea 18

Home Missionaries

Children's workers often miss out on participation in adult Bible studies and fellowship groups in order to work with the kids. Help them stay in contact by creating an attractive poster or bulletin board in one or more of the adult classrooms. Title the board "Home Missionaries from Our Class," and include a close-up photo of each teacher or helper who calls that class "home." (You may want to assign some workers to appropriate classrooms if they do not already belong to an adult group.)

Ask each adult class to pray for their home missionaries every week. Have the class drop a note from time to time to encourage the workers, just as they would do for any other missionary they support. Encourage class leaders to keep the home missionaries informed of socials and other special events.

Bonus Idea 19

Praying With Your Teachers

Have a place and a time set aside before each program to meet and pray with your teachers and helpers. Or have a pastor or church leader stop by each classroom just before the kids arrive and take a moment to pray for each volunteer.

Bonus Idea 20

Happy Birthday!

Ask new teachers and helpers for their birth dates when they join your team. Keep track of these special dates on a calendar or computerized database.

At the end of each month, write quick, easy "Happy Birthday" postcards to all of the workers having birthdays in the next month. You can use Love Note 10 (p. 91). Put their actual birth dates where the stamps would go, and keep the stack by your phone. Each Monday morning, add stamps to the ones for that week and drop them in the mail.

It's simple, effective, and affirming!

Bonus Idea 21

Happy Anniversary!

Follow the procedure from Bonus Idea 20, but keep track of your staff's wedding anniversaries. If an anniversary falls on a Sunday, give the couple a day off by providing a teacher substitute (or two, if both spouses work in the children's ministry).

6

READY-to-COPY LOVE NOTES FOR PEOPLE WHO LOVE KIDS

Here's an easy way to show your love and appreciation for the teachers and helpers who minister to kids at your church week in and week out: Send them a "Love Note"! Print a bunch of these postcard-sized notes, pre-stamp them, and keep them in your desk, along with a roster of your volunteers' names and addresses. They'll be there, ready for you to drop in the mail, whenever you need to encourage a worker!

The photocopiable Love Notes in this section have been designed to fit four cards on an 8½ x 11 sheet of card stock. Copy the originals from this book at 100 percent to ensure the cards are the right size to meet U.S. Postal Service requirements for postcard size. Make your own masters, four to a page, and then ask your local print shop or photocopy store to print them with colored ink on a nicely contrasting color of card stock. (Watch for in-store specials on color copies!) They can also cut the cards for you.

The Postal Service has specific requirements for minimum and maximum dimensions of postcards. With the sizes we've recommended, you can mail your Love Notes at the reduced first-class postcard rate. If the postcards are too small, the post office will not accept them; if they're too large, they may require regular first-class postage. (For more information, size restrictions, and current postal rates, call the post office toll free at 1-800-275-8777.)

"I thank my God every time I remember you. In all my prayers for all of you, I always pray with joy because of your partnership in the gospel from the first day until now"

(Philippians 1:3-5).

"Jesus said…'Go and make disciples of all nations, baptizing them in the name of the Father and of the Son and of the Holy Spirit, and teaching them to obey everything I have commanded you' "

(Matthew 28:18-20).

Thanks for obeying Jesus as you help to make disciples of kids at our church. Let's keep working together to fulfill the Great Commission.

Love Note 3 instructions: Encourage your male teachers or teen helpers by attaching this card to a baseball, a Wiffle ball, or a wrapped chocolate baseball and presenting it to them in their classrooms. Add a note on the reverse side specifying the "something wonderful."

I caught you...

...doing something wonderful!

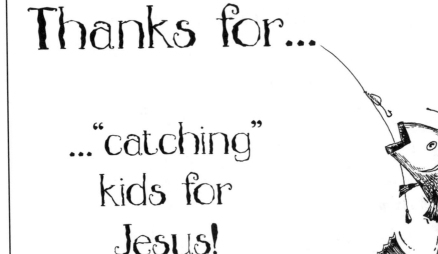

Thanks for...

..."catching" kids for Jesus!

Love Note 4 instructions: Attach a fishing hook, gummy fish, or bag of gummy worms to this card and present it to your nature-loving teachers to encourage and thank them for their ministry. Add a note on the back affirming one action that you observed them doing.

Love Note 5 instructions: Encourage your female teachers and helpers by attaching a wrapped choco-late heart or a box of conversation hearts to this card and presenting it to them when they least expect it.

You have a heart for kids!

And your ministry is close to God's own heart.

You gave me such JOY when I saw you:

- ❏ Changing the babies' diapers so lovingly.
- ❏ Holding and giving love to a crying child.
- ❏ Dealing with an upset parent with patience and gentleness.
- ❏ Caring for another teacher in our ministry.
- ❏ All of the above!

Love Note 6 instructions: Attach an Almond Joy candy bar and mark off the appropriate comments. Hand this treat to a deserving worker on a Sunday morning!

Love Note 7 instructions: Attach a candle or light bulb to this card, and share it with a teacher who really "brightens up" your program.

THANKS FOR LETTING YOUR LIGHT SHINE!

You're making a difference for eternity.

Thanks for making us all
SNICKER.

(Kids learn best when they're having fun!)

Love Note 8 instructions: Attach a Snickers candy bar to the card and present it to someone at a teacher training meeting. Or affirm a particularly fun teacher by awarding this on a Sunday morning.

Love Note 9 instructions: Use this card to remind your teachers and helpers of the next staff meeting. Attach a honey packet from a local fast-food restaurant, a piece of Bit-O-Honey candy, or a sample-sized box of Honey-Comb cereal to make it really memorable!

God's Word is sweeter than honey...and so are you! Come to our Children's Ministry team meeting this month!

Date: _____

Time: _____

Location: _____

Happy Birthday!

"Praise be to the God and Father of our Lord Jesus Christ! In his great mercy he has given us new birth into a living hope through the resurrection of Jesus Christ from the dead, and into an inheritance that can never perish, spoil or fade—kept in heaven for you" (1 Peter 1:3-4).

Let's Celebrate!

Love Note 10

Knowing you'll be at Sunday school is the highlight of some child's week.

You're affecting a child's eternity and his entire view of church and God! Thanks for ministering so faithfully.

TEACHERS UNLOCK THE JOY AND MYSTERY OF GOD'S WORD FOR KIDS.

YOU'RE "KEY" TO THE MINISTRY OF OUR CHURCH!

Love Note 12 instructions: See Bonus Idea 11 (p. 81) for ideas about using this postcard.

Love Note 13 instructions: Attach a spice tea bag, a cinnamon stick, or a small bottle of cooking spices. Or attach a small bottle of Tabasco sauce, chili seasoning, or a small bag of red-hot candies. You might use this to encourage your most "seasoned" veterans!

THANKS FOR
SPICING
UP OUR MINISTRY
TO KIDS!

You're writing

God's Word on the

hearts of children.

Thanks for your ministry!

You're so good that your kids always get the point!

Love Note 14 instructions: Sharpen two new pencils. Attach one to the top of the card, the other to the bottom. Use this to congratulate a teacher who has just led a child to become a Christian!

MARY HAD A LITTLE LAMB...
HIS NAME WAS JESUS!

"JESUS SAID, 'FEED MY SHEEP' " (John 21:17).

MERRY CHRISTMAS, AND THANK YOU
FOR SHEPHERDING KIDS AT OUR CHURCH!

"Go quickly and tell his children: He has risen from the dead"
(Matthew 28:7, paraphrased).

Happy Easter!

He is risen! He is risen indeed!

SCRipTURe InDeX

Group Publishing, Inc.
Attention: Product Development
P.O. Box 481
Loveland, CO 80539
Fax: (970) 679-4370

Evaluation for *DEVOTIONS FOR PEOPLE WHO LOVE KIDS*

Please help Group Publishing, Inc., continue to provide innovative and useful resources for ministry. Please take a moment to fill out this evaluation and mail or fax it to us. Thanks!

● ● ●

1. As a whole, this book has been (circle one)

not very helpful   very helpful

1   2   3   4   5   6   7   8   9   10

2. The best things about this book:

3. Ways this book could be improved:

4. Things I will change because of this book:

5. Other books I'd like to see Group publish in the future:

6. Would you be interested in field-testing future Group products and giving us your feedback? If so, please fill in the information below:

Name _____

Street Address _____

City _____ State _____ ZIP _____

Phone Number _____ Date _____